ON POETS
AND
OTHERS

Joan —
May you enjoy Paz's
essays as much as his
poetry. Happy 33rd
Birthday!

Cheers! Heidi

TITLES BY OCTAVIO PAZ
AVAILABLE FROM ARCADE PUBLISHING

Alternating Current
Conjunctions and Disjunctions
Marcel Duchamp: Appearance Stripped Bare
The Monkey Grammarian
On Poets and Others

OCTAVIO PAZ

ON POETS
AND
OTHERS

Translated from the Spanish by
MICHAEL SCHMIDT

ARCADE PUBLISHING • NEW YORK

Little, Brown and Company

First Arcade Edition 1990

Some of the material in this volume has appeared previously in the following publications: *In/Mediaciones,* 1979; *Plural* 30, March 1974; *Plural* 51, December 1975; *El Pais,* 1980; *Alternating Current,* 1967; *Sur,* July 1943; *El Arcoyla Cira,* 1956; *Poetry Nation,* 1975.

ISBN 1-55970-139-0

Library of Congress Cataloging-in-Publication information is available.

Published in the United States by Arcade Publishing, Inc., New York, a Little, Brown company, by arrangement with Seaver Books

10 9 8 7 6 5 4 3 2 1

M A R

Design by Beth Tondreau

Published simultaneously in Canada by Little, Brown & Company (Canada) Limited

Printed in the United States of America

CONTENTS

CONTENTS

FOREWORD

When you meet Octavio Paz, you have the impression you're meeting *all* of him. He seems to contain all his ages. There is about him, and about the way he moves and laughs, often at himself, something of the adolescent. Here is the student striding through the streets of Mexico City at night arguing politics, discussing Dostoevski, with his schoolmates, joining the student strike in 1929. Here, too is the young idealist who went to the Yucatan in his early twenties to help found a school for the children of the sisal workers; and then went to Spain during the Civil War. Paz is recognizably the young disciple of the surrealist André Breton; and he retains the charismatic luster of controversial diplomat and teacher. Paz doesn't repudiate his past, and, unlike Nietzsche—whom he admires, and who systematically refused to revise his early work because, as he put it, "the young man he had been would have despised the older man he had become"—Paz is often willing to revise work he wrote four decades ago. It may be that poems are never finished, only abandoned—but still, Paz returns to some of them, drawing them a little farther along the road.

In many of the essays contained in this collection, Paz describes the relations of this young man—himself—with his elder and more established writers and philosophers. Robert Frost, Luis Cernuda, José Ortega y Gasset, William Carlos Williams, Ezra Pound, André Breton, all appear here to have been influences in Paz's life. In each of them he finds something to build on. And if ultimately he rejects them all, it is ruefully, an almost filial estrangement. Octavio Paz is a "pluralist." One of his favorite critical terms is *pluralism* in culture. Paz is deeply rooted in the cultures of the Spanish language. The poets and philosophers of France and England marked him, as did the various cultures and overwhelming erotic art of India. In each he finds ways of understanding his own culture. They show him different routes back to the beginning. French lucidity, even in revolution; English continuity, despite changes of the world outside; Indian mysticism, especially the mysticism of the body—all these help Paz home, to himself and his own culture, overlaid as it is by patterns of violence and repression.

Writing at the time of Breton's death, Paz notes: "All of us who had anything to do with Breton experienced a dual, dizzying feeling: fascination and a centrifugal impulse. I confess that for a long time I was kept awake by the worry that I might do or say something to provoke his reproof. I believe many of his friends had a similar experience. . . . I should say that I write as if I were engaged in a silent dialogue with Breton: reply, answer, coincidence, disagreement, homage, all together. Even as I write this I experience that feeling." Under Breton's influence, Paz tried automatic writing and produced his great prose-poems. But it's interesting that in his valedictory essay on Breton, Paz quotes none of his master's poetry, only his critical statements. The English critic Jason Wilson suggests that Breton was an influence on Paz's poetics more than on the poetry itself, and I suspect he's right. In Paz there is a double impulse: first, an enthusiasm for ideas, especially ideas about poetry and poetic traditions. He is brilliant at recounting the history of artistic trends of this and last century, the modernist "tradition of discontinuity" called up in the titles of books such as *Conjunctions and Disjunctions* and *Alternating Current*. But at the other pole of his imaginative thought, T. S. Eliot has left a deep mark on his work. Eliot is in almost every way the opposite of Breton. Paz rejects Eliot's religion and politics; but he can't resist the actual poems and the literary essays.

Like other radical writers before him, Paz locates the intellectual poverty of much of Latin America in the fact that the eighteenth century—the great critical century, the Enlightenment—passed it by. While the United States was colonized by the spirit of the Reformation, Latin America suffered the Counter-Reformation. Without an Enlightenment, the critical disciplines that developed in France and England were not practiced in the Spanish colonies. Paz provides some benefits of the Enlightenment for Latin America. He is not alone in this, and he doesn't set out to write like Voltaire. But he produces social and literary criticism—for him the two are inseparable—which he has set in the French tradition of "moralism."

His most famous prose book is *The Labyrinth of Solitude*, published in 1950 and revised in 1959. In it he explores the Mexican psyche and tries to place Mexican history back within the Mexican himself. As he put it in an interview a decade ago, he wanted to "recover the consciousness" of a country that history had pushed aside. "One of the pivotal ideas of the book," he said, "is that there is a Mexico which is buried but alive. Or, more accurately, there is in Mexican men and women a universe of buried images, desires and impulses. I attempted a description—inadequate of course, little more than a glimpse—of the world of repressions, inhibitions, memories, appetites and dreams which Mexico has been and is." *The Labyrinth of Solitude* has fascinated two intellectual generations in Latin America. It is one of those rare keys to a culture that usually seems to be written by critics from the outside. Paz's rare achievement was to write as an insider, with passion *and* detachment. He has said, "Already at that time I thought as I do now, that history is a form of knowledge set between science properly speaking and poetry. Historical knowledge is not quantitative nor can the historian discover historical laws. The historian describes things like a scientist and has visions like a poet." His "history" is not in chronological sequence. Paz brings facts and images to the foreground and holds them still while he examines them minutely, tracing their origins, discovering their latencies. There are elements of autobiography in the images chosen. When Paz writes about the rituals for the day of the dead, the little offerings of sugar, clay, and raffia are peculiarly vivid. He grew up near where these things were made and as a child strayed among the craftsmen's workshops. The relations between such images and the beliefs they reveal are teased out, now lovingly, now angrily. When Paz distinguishes firmly between ideas and beliefs, he follows his philosophical teacher José Ortega y Gasset. Ideas are changeable, in movement; beliefs are largely static and constant. "A man is defined more by what he believes than by what he thinks," Paz says. Paz *partly* believes, and in this he is typical of many modern writers. There is a withholding which is painful because the writer remains at the crossroads, his journey forever incomplete.

Skepticism and openness make it possible for Paz to see his world and his history freshly. Since the wars of independence, Latin Americans have tended to despise the earlier colonial periods. Paz emphasizes the decades of relative plenty and stability and the great cultural achievement of the colony. He underlines the political balances of power that existed between church and state. His aim isn't to apologize for the colonial system, but to restore a balance in our perception, to counter the automatic rhetoric that prevails in teaching and writing. Until the colonial period is integrated into the memory of Latin Americans, an essential part of the past remains repressed.

In *The Labyrinth of Solitude* Paz makes another unpopular point. He insists on the place of the brutal Emiliano Zapata in the Mexican Revolution, but he assigns to him an unexpected destiny. Zapata's project was an "attempt to return to origins." According to Paz, "the paradox of Zapatismo was that it was a profoundly traditionalist movement; and precisely in that traditionalism its revolutionary might resides. To put it more clearly, because it was traditionalist, Zapatismo was radically subversive." Zapata becomes for Paz a political talisman for his own poetic quest of *return*. Zapata's movement "signifies revelation, the emergence of certain hidden and repressed realities. It is revolution not as ideology but as an instinctive movement, an explosion which is the revelation of a reality prior to hierarchies, classes, property." I think the phrase "revolution not as ideology" is the key to his political writing.

In 1936, the Chilean poet Pablo Neruda arranged for Octavio Paz to go to Spain at the time of the Civil War. In Spain Paz did not like what he saw of the machinations of the Popular Front and its patrons. He began to question his kind of Marxist allegiances. His doubts were heightened by the Nazi-Soviet pact and later by his estrangement from Neruda. Ideological politics became for him the great seduction and the great tragedy of the writers of this and the last century. "The history of modern literature, from the German and English romantics to our own days, is the history of a long, unhappy passion for politics. From Coleridge to Mayakovski, Revolution has been the great Goddess, the eternal beloved and the great whore to poets and novelists. Politics filled Malraux's head with smoke, poisoned the sleepless nights of Cesar Vallejo, killed García Lorca, abandoned the old

poet Antonio Machado in a village in the Pyrenees, locked Pound
in an asylum, dishonoured Neruda and Aragon, has made Sartre
a figure of ridicule, and has acknowledged Breton all too late.
But we can't disown politics; it would be worse than spitting at
the sky, spitting at ourselves." In one of his finest poems, the
"Nocturne of San Ildefonso," he writes:

> The good, we sought the good:
>   to straighten out the world.
> We did not lack integrity:
>   we lacked humility.
> What we wanted we wanted without innocence.

His bitterness is hardly surprising. While Paz is a highly respected
and loved poet, he remains a figure of controversy, and that
controversy is political. The Latin American intellectual world is
largely committed to the left in rather old-fashioned ways. And
Paz represents another kind of radicalism. He began to define it
when he published an article in the Argentinean magazine *Sur*,
edited by Victoria Ocampo. She was the only editor brave enough
to print it back in 1951. The article was on the Soviet labor
camps. Paz had been collecting information about them with
growing horror. If socialism was to claim any moral authority,
it would have urgently to come to terms with the aberrations of
Stalinism. When the piece appeared, Paz anticipated debate. In-
stead, it was greeted with public silence and with private abuse.
Neruda was prominent among his accusers. He was "giving am-
munition to the enemy"—namely the United States. Better sup-
press the truth, common sense said. Paz writes in the same poem,

> Poetry,
>   the bridge suspended between history and truth,
> is not a way towards this or that:
>   it is to see
> the stillness within movement.

In those lines he says something with which few of his fellow Latin American poets would agree. He refuses to put his art to use.

He remains a radical, but a radical who rejects ideologies. Paz sees his task in these terms: "The writer should be a sniper, he should endure solitude, he should know himself to be a marginal being. It is both a curse and a blessing that we writers are marginal." He also says: "Criticism is the apprenticeship of the revising imagination—imagination cured of fantasy and resolved to confront the world's reality. Criticism tells us that we ought to learn to dissolve the idols, learn to dissolve them in ourselves. We have to learn to be air, dream set free." This is no recipe for passivity. Paz has learned his own lesson. "Criticism reveals the possibility of liberty and this is an invitation to action." The failure of democracy in Latin America is a failure of criticism. Technological progress without a critical capacity gives us "more things, not more being."

Criticism is a discipline that keeps language to its meanings. "When a society becomes corrupt," he writes, "what first grows gangrenous is language. Social criticism, therefore, begins with grammar and the reestablishment of meanings." Even so, the true writer has an uneasy relationship with his language. For Paz the natural metaphor is an erotic one: "I believe the writer's attitude to language should be that of a lover: fidelity and, at the same time, a lack of respect for the beloved object. Veneration and transgression."

Opposite this caring and necessarily violent lover, he identifies the enemy—the enemy both of the individual and of the collective: the bureaucratic state perverted by ideology. This state he defines as *The Philanthropic Ogre* in one of his books of political essays: a cold, totalitarian monster that devours its children without appetite, mechanically, chewing hard.

Octavio Paz came up hard against that ogre at the end of his diplomatic career. From 1962 to 1968 he was Mexican ambassador to India. In 1968, the Olympic Games were staged in Mexico City, and radical students assembled huge demonstrations. One of them ended in a massacre—no one is quite sure how many people were killed. This outrage revealed to Paz what he had long suspected—the inability of the Mexican system to respond to democratic pressure. The written constitution remained a luminous fiction, the rhetoric of politics grew increasingly remote from the huge, hungry, unemployed sub-proletariat that had swamped the major cities. He could no longer represent the Mexican government. His resignation had considerable political effect. He spoke later of the "vitiated intellectual atmosphere" of Mexico. "Among us," he declared, "ideological simplifications dominate and our intellectuals do not show much respect for reality."

When he returned to Mexico two years later, he was a painful thorn in the side of the political establishment. But increasingly he also became an irritant to radical intellectuals. After his resignation he had been vested with great authority. Now he rejected the popular accolade and preferred to continue on his own way. His critical essays have not made comfortable reading for anyone. During the last ten years he has alienated many people in my generation and in the one before. They tend to see Paz as someone who has taken the conventional journey from left to right. They say his early work exceeds his later work in scope and quality. But for younger writers he is once again clearly a teacher and guide. He makes himself available, he encourages their work, he is a genuine solitary radical, a man in search of roots, and he responds to evidence of that search in others.

To be sure, the best early poems are major; but it is in the more recent collections and long poems, where he traces his way back through his culture, that he accomplishes what he set out to do over half a century ago. He carries less cultural luggage now—memory has done its sifting and what remains is the essential, the unforgettable, the things of which he is himself made.

When he stepped away from political in-fighting and stood alone, he found his great subject not only in his Mexico's past but in his own. His life has spanned years of critical change in Latin America. He has seen the ends of a dozen dreams and his beloved cities dehumanized by overcrowding, pollution, destitution, almost as tragically as the cities of India. It is the end not only of dreams but of cultures and communities; in such places, how can the dream be set free?

Through his father and grandfather, Paz has the next best thing to a firsthand memory of nineteenth-century Mexico, when liberalism triumphed for a time. During this time the tensions which distort present-day Mexico did not exist. His most recent magazine is *Vuelta*, one of the most influential journals in Latin America. He is a wonderfully imaginative editor, one who invites into the Mexican arena an incongruous and stimulating range of intelligences from Europe and the rest of his own continent. For him, no subject is taboo. The title of the magazine implies turn, return, or turning back. His last major collection of poems, published in 1974, is also entitled *Vuelta*. In Emiliano Zapata, André Breton, and the writers and artists he admires, and in the religious and erotic traditions he explored during his years in India, he is looking for origins, sources, and the fresh resources that flow from them.

He spent his childhood in the village of Mixcoac, a suburb of Mexico City. It has an Aztec name and some broken walls survive from pre-conquest times. If you scratch about in your garden there you sometimes find potsherds. There are also colonial buildings—nothing very striking, but solid and permanent. There are examples of later architecture, too, and an inner ring road that reminds you that this is 1986 and nothing is safe against the ravages of technology. Nothing except memory and the sensitive eye registering its place in this visual anthology of popular Mexican history. Octavio Paz's grandfather, Ireneo, dominated the house where he grew up. Ireneo was a lawyer and a liberal reformer who fought against the French and wrote more than ten books. He edited a daily paper for thirty-eight years. To Paz the child, he was an old and disheartened man. He had fallen in, probably reluctantly, behind the strong man—the dictator Porfirio Díaz—and his cause was defeated by the revolution. Octavio Paz's father rebelled against Ireneo. Liberalism had failed. He supported something more radical, the revolution, and especially the agrarian reform which Zapata stood for. He was an agent and then a propagandist for Zapata. When the poet was a boy, old Zapatistas used to visit, bringing delicious, strange foods from their pueblos. They made a marked impression on the boy: they seemed to contain the turbulent history he was too young to remember. Paz's father, who became an alcoholic, died tragically in a train crash in 1935.

> My father went and came back through the flames.
>
> Among the sleepers and the rails
>   of a station swarming with flies and dust
> One afternoon we gathered up his pieces.
>   I was never able to speak with him.
> I find him now in dreams.
> That half-erased country of the dead.

The poet's mother was a Mexican of Spanish background. She was not cultured, but she was affectionate and supportive. He speaks of her tenderly as "a love letter with errors in the grammar."

In my opinion, his finest poem is "Pasado en Claro" which means "Fair Draft" or, as a translator has it, "A Draft of Shadows"; it was published in 1975. The energy of the language and the imaginative penetration of this poem set it in a class by itself. It evokes the long history of ritual, repression, and change in Mexico, but also Paz's own life, which in this context becomes ours as much as Wordsworth's does in *The Prelude*. He declares a debt to Wordsworth not only in the way the poem works but in the epigraph:

> Fair seed-time had my soul, and I grew up
> Foster'd alike by beauty and by fear.

Beauty and fear. In a sense, they are the twin poles not only of Paz's life but also of his work.

—MICHAEL SCHMIDT

ON POETS
AND
OTHERS

ROBERT FROST: VISIT TO A POET

After twenty minutes walking along the highway under a three o'clock sun, I came at last to the turning. I veered right and began to climb the slope. At intervals, the trees along the path provided a little coolness. Water ran down a small brook, through the undergrowth. The sand squeaked under my tread. Sun was everywhere. In the air there was a scent of green, hot growth, thirsty. Not a tree, not a leaf stirred. A few clouds rested heavily, anchored in a blue, waveless gulf. A bird sang. I hesitated: "How much nicer it would be to stretch out under this elm! The sound of water is worth more than all the poets' words." I walked on for another ten minutes. When I got to the farm, some fair-haired children were playing around a birch tree. I asked for the master; without interrupting their game, they replied, "He's up there, in the cabin." And they pointed to the very summit of the hill. I set off again. Now I was walking through deep undergrowth that came up to my knee. When I reached the top I could see the whole little valley; the blue mountains, the stream, the luminously green flatland, and, at the very bottom, the forest. The wind began to blow; everything swayed, almost cheerfully. All the leaves sang. I went toward the cabin. It was a little wooden shack, old, the paint flaked, grayed by the years. The windows were curtainless; I made a way through the underbrush and looked in. Inside, sitting in an easy chair, was an old man. Resting beside him was a woolly dog. When he saw me the man stood up and beckoned me to come around the other side. I did so and found him waiting for me at the door of his cabin. The dog jumped up to greet me. We crossed a little passage and went into a small room: unpolished floor, two chairs, a blue easy chair, another reddish one, a desk with a few books on it, a little table with papers and letters. On the walls three or four engravings, nothing remarkable. We sat down.

"Sure is hot. You want a beer?"

"Yes, I believe I do. I've walked half an hour and I'm worn out."

We drank the beer slowly. While I sipped mine, I took him in. With his white shirt open—is there anything cleaner than a clean white shirt?—his eyes blue, innocent, ironic, his philosopher's head and his farmer's hands, he looked like an ancient sage, the kind who prefers to observe the world from his retreat. But there was nothing ascetic in his looks, rather a manly sobriety. There he was, in his cabin, removed from the world, not to renounce it but to see it better. He wasn't a hermit nor was his hill a rock in the desert. The three crows hadn't brought him the bread he ate; he'd bought it himself in the village store.

"It's really a beautiful place. It almost seems real. This landscape is very different from ours in Mexico, it's made for men to look at. The distances are made for our legs, too."

"My daughter's told me the landscape of your country's very dramatic."

"Nature is hostile down there. What's more, we're few and weak. Man is consumed by the landscape and there's always the danger you might turn into a cactus."

"They tell me that men sit still for hours there just doing nothing."

"Afternoons you see them, completely still, by the roadsides or at the entrances to towns."

"Is that how they do their thinking?"

"It's a country that's going to turn to stone one day. The trees and the plants all tend to stone, just as the men do. And the animals, too: dogs, coyotes, snakes. There are little baked clay birds and it's very strange to see them fly and hear them sing, because you never get used to the idea they're real birds."

"When I was fifteen I wrote a poem. My first poem. And you know what it was about? *La noche triste*. I was reading Prescott then, and maybe reading him set me thinking about your country. Have you read Prescott?"

"That was one of my grandfather's favorite books, so I read him when I was a boy. I'd like to read him again."

"I like rereading books, too. I don't trust folk who don't reread. And those who read a lot of books. It seems crazy to me, this modern madness, and it'll only increase the number of pedants. You've got to read a few books well and frequently."

"A friend tells me they've invented a way of developing speed-reading. I think they're planning to introduce it into schools."

"They're mad. What you've got to teach people is to read slowly. And not to fidget about so much. And do you know why they invent all these things? Because they're scared. People are scared to pause on things, because that compromises them. That's why they flee the country and move to the cities. They're scared of being by themselves."

"Yes, the world's full of fear."

"And those with power exploit that fear. Individual life has never been so despised or authority so revered."

"Sure, it's easier to live as one, to decide as one. Even dying's easier, if you die at someone else's expense. We're invaded by fear. There's the common man's fear, and he hands himself over to the strong man. But there's also the fear the powerful feel; they don't dare to stay alone. Because they're scared, they cling onto power."

"Here people abandon the country to go work in factories. And when they come back they don't like the country anymore. The country's hard. You've always got to be alert, and you're responsible for everything and not just for a part, like in a factory."

"What's more, the country's the experience of solitude. You can't go to the films, or take refuge in a bar."

"Exactly. It's the experience of being free. It's like poetry. Life's like poetry, when the poet writes a poem. It begins as an invitation to the unknown: the first line gets written and what's to follow is unknown. It's unsure whether in the next line poetry's waiting for us, or failure. And that sense of mortal danger accompanies the poet in all his adventures."

"In each verse a decision awaits us, and we can't choose to close our eyes and let instinct work on its own. Poetic instinct consists of an alert tension."

"In each line, in each phrase the possibility of failure is concealed. The possibility that the whole poem, not just that isolated verse, will fail. That's how life is: at every moment we can lose it. Every moment there's mortal risk. Each instant is a choice."

"You're right. Poetry is the experience of liberty. The poet risks himself, chances all on the poem's all with each verse he writes."

"And you can't change your mind. Each act, each verse is

4

irrevocable, forever. In each verse one is committed forever. But now folks have become irresponsible. No one wants to decide for himself. Like those poets who copy their ancestors."

"Don't you believe in the tradition?"

"Yes, but each poet's born to express something that's his own. And his first duty is to deny his ancestors, the rhetoric of those who've come before. When I started writing I found that the words of the old writers were no use to me; it was necessary for me to create my own language. And that language—which surprised and troubled some people—was the language of my community, the language that surrounded my childhood and adolescence. I had to wait a long time before I found my words. You've got to use everyday language. . . ."

"But subjected to a different pressure. As if each word had been created only to express that particular moment. Because there's a certain fatality in words; a French writer says that 'images can't be looked for, they're found.' I don't think he means that chance presides over creation but that a *fated choice* leads us to certain words."

"The poet creates his own language. Then he ought to fight against *that* rhetoric. He should never abandon himself to his style."

"There are no poetic styles. When you get to style, literature displaces poetry."

"That was the case with American poetry when I started writing. That's where all my difficulties and my successes began. And now maybe it's necessary to fight against the rhetoric we've made. The world goes round and what was in yesterday is out today. You've got to make a little fun of all this. No need to take anything too seriously, not even ideas. Or rather, precisely because we're so serious and passionate, we ought to laugh at ourselves a little. Don't trust those who don't know how to laugh."

And he laughed with the laughter of a man who has seen rain, and also of a man who has got wet. We got up and went out for a little walk. We went down the hill. The dog leapt ahead of us. As we came out, he said to me:

"Most of all, don't trust those who don't know how to laugh at themselves. Solemn poets, humorless professors, prophets who only know how to howl and harangue. All those dangerous men."

"Do you read the contemporaries?"

"I always read poetry. I like reading the poems of young writers. And some philosophers. But I can't stand novels. I don't think I've ever read one through."

We walked on. When we got to the farmhouse, the children gathered round us. The poet was now telling me about his childhood, the years in San Francisco, and his return to New England.

"This is my country and I believe this is where the nation has its roots. Everything grew from here. Do you know that the state of Vermont refused to participate in the war against Mexico? Yes, everything grew from here. This is where the desire to immerse oneself in the unknown began, and the desire to stay alone with yourself. We ought to go back to that if we want to preserve what we are."

"It seems pretty hard to me. You're now a rich people."

"Years ago I thought of going to a little country, where the noise that everyone makes just isn't heard. I chose Costa Rica; when I was getting ready to go I learned that there too an American company called the tune. I didn't go. That's why I'm here, in New England."

We came to the turning. I looked at my watch: more than two hours had passed.

"I'd better be going. They're waiting for me down below, in Bread Loaf."

He stretched out his hand.

"You know the way?"

"Yes," I said, and we shook hands. When I'd gone a few steps I heard his voice:

"Come back soon! And when you get to New York, write to me. Don't forget."

I answered with a nod. I saw him climbing the path playing with his dog. "And he's seventy years old," I thought. As I walked back, I remembered another loner, another visit. "I think Robert Frost would like to have known Antonio Machado. But how would they have understood each other? The Spaniard didn't speak English, and the American doesn't know Spanish. No matter, they would have smiled. I'm sure they would have made friends straightaway." I remembered the house at Rocafort, in Valencia, the wild, neglected garden, the living room and the dust-covered furniture. And Machado, the cigarette in his mouth gone out. The Spaniard was also an old man retired from the world, and he too knew how to laugh and he too was absent-minded. Like the American, he liked to philosophize, not in the schools but at the periphery. Sages for the people; the American in his cabin, the Spaniard in his provincial café. Machado too expressed a horror of the solemn and had the same smiling gravity. "Yes, the Anglo-Saxon has the cleaner shirt and there are more trees in his view. But the other's smile was sadder and finer. There's a great deal of snow in this fellow's poems, but there's dust, antiquity, history in the other's. That dust of Castile, that dust of Mexico, which as soon as you touch it dissolves between your hands. . . ."

Vermont, June 1945

WALT WHITMAN

Walt Whitman is the only great modern poet who does not seem to experience discord when he faces his world. Not even solitude; his monologue is a universal chorus. No doubt there are at least two people in him: the public poet and the private person who conceals his true erotic inclinations. But the mask—that of the poet of democracy—is rather more than a mask; it is his true face. Despite certain recent interpretations, in Whitman the poetic and the historical dream come together. There is no gap between his beliefs and social reality. And this fact is more important—I mean, more widely pertinent and significant—than any psychological consideration. The uniqueness of Whitman's poetry in the modern world cannot be explained except as a function of another, even greater, uniqueness which includes it: that of America.

In a book* which is a model of its genre, Edmundo O'Gorman has shown that our continent was never discovered. In effect, it is impossible to discover something which does not exist, and America, before its so-called discovery, did not exist. One ought rather to speak of the *invention* of America than of its discovery. If America is a creation of the European spirit, it begins to emerge from the sea-mists centuries before the expeditions of Columbus. And what the Europeans discover when they reach these lands is their own historic dream. Reyes has devoted some lucid pages to this subject: America is a sudden embodiment of a European utopia. The dream becomes a reality, a present; America is a present: a gift, a given of history. But it is an open present, a today that is tinged with tomorrow. The presence and the present of America are a future; our continent is, by its nature, the land which does not exist on its own, but as something which is created and invented. Its being, its reality or substance, consists of being always future, history which is justified not by the past but by what is to come. Our foundation is not what America was but what it will be. America never was; and *it is, only if it is utopia*, history on its way to a golden age.

This may not be entirely true if one considers the colonial period of Spanish and Portuguese America. But it is revealing how, just as soon as the Latin Americans acquire self-consciousness and oppose the Spaniards, they rediscover the utopian nature of America and make the French utopias their own. All of them see in wars of independence a return to first principles, a reversion to what America really is. The War of Independence is a correction of American history and, as such, a restoration of the original reality. The exceptional and genuinely paradoxical nature of this restoration becomes clear if one notes that it consists of a restoration of the future. Thanks to French revolutionary principles,

---

*La idea del descubrimiento de America (1951)

Latin America becomes again what it was at its birth: not a past, but a future, a dream. The dream of Europe, the place of choice, spatial and temporal, of all that the European reality could not be except by denying itself and its past. America is the dream of Europe, now free of European history, free of the burden of tradition. Once the problem of independence is resolved, the abstract and utopian nature of liberal America begins to show again in episodes such as the French intervention in Mexico. Neither Juárez nor his soldiers ever believed—according to Cosío Villegas—that they fought against France, but against a French usurpation. The true France was ideal and universal and more than just a nation, it was an idea, a philosophy. Cuesta says, with some justice, that the war with the French should be seen as a "civil war." It needed the Mexican Revolution to wake the country from this philosophical dream—which, in another way, concealed an historical reality hardly touched upon by the Independence, the Reform, and the Dictatorship—and discover itself, no longer as an abstract future but as an origin in which the three times needed to be sought: our past, our present, our future. The historical emphasis changed tense, and in this consists the true spiritual significance of the Mexican Revolution.

The utopian character of America is even purer in the Saxon portion of the continent. There were no complex Indian cultures there, nor did Roman Catholicism erect its vast nontemporal structures: America was—if it was anything—geography, pure space, open to human action. Lacking historical substance—old class divisions, ancient institutions, inherited beliefs and laws— reality presented only natural obstacles. Men fought, not against history, but against nature. And where there was an historical obstacle—as in the Indian societies—it was erased from history and, reduced to a mere act of nature, action followed as if this were so. The North American attitude can be condemned in these terms: all that does not have a part in the utopian nature of America does not properly belong to history: it is a natural event and, thus, it doesn't exist; or it exists only as an inert obstacle, not as an alien conscience. Evil is outside, part of the natural world—like Indians, rivers, mountains, and other obstacles which must be domesticated or destroyed; or it is an intrusive reality (the English past, Spanish Catholicism, monarchy, etc.). The American War of Independence is the expulsion of the intrusive elements, alien to the American essence. If American reality is the reinvention of itself, whatever is found in any way irreducible or unassimilable is not American. In other places the future is a human attribute: because we are men, we have a future; in the Anglo-Saxon America of the last century, the process is inverted and the future determines man: we are men because we have a future. And whatever has no future is not man. Thus, reality leaves no gap at all for contradiction, ambiguity, or conflict to appear.

Whitman can sing confidently and in blithe innocence about democracy militant because the American utopia is confused with and indistinguishable from American reality. Whitman's poetry is a great prophetic dream, but it is a dream within another even greater one that feeds it. America is dreamed in Whitman's poetry because it is a dream itself. And it is dreamed as a concrete reality, almost a *physical* reality, with its men, its rivers, its cities and mountains. All that huge mass of reality moves lightly, as if it were weightless; and in fact, it is without historic weight: it is the future incarnate. The reality Whitman sings is utopian. By this I do not mean that it is unreal or exists only as idea, but that its essence, what enlivens it, justifies and makes sense of its progress and gives weight to its movements, is the future. Dream within a dream, Whitman's poetry is realistic only on this count: his dream is the dream of the reality itself, which has no other substance but to invent itself and dream itself. "When we dream that we dream," Novalis says, "waking is near at hand." Whitman was never aware that he dreamed and always thought himself a poetic realist. And he was, but only insofar as the reality

11

he celebrated was not something given, but a substance crossed and recrossed by the future.

America dreams itself in Whitman because it was itself a dream, pure creation. Before and since Whitman we have had other poetic dreams. All of them—whether the dreamer's name is Poe or Darío, Melville or Dickinson—are more like attempts to escape from the American nightmare.

Mexico, 1956

WILLIAM CARLOS WILLIAMS: THE SAXIFRAGE FLOWER

for James Laughlin

In the first third of our century, a change occurred in the literatures of the English language which affected verse and prose, syntax and sensibility, imagination and prosody alike. The change— similar to those which occurred about the same time in other parts of Europe and in Latin America—was originally the work of a handful of poets, almost all of them Americans. In that group of founders, William Carlos Williams occupies a place at once central and unique: unlike Pound and Eliot, he preferred to bury himself in a little city outside New York rather than uproot himself and go to London or Paris; unlike Wallace Stevens and e. e. cummings, who also decided to stay in the United States but who were cosmopolitan spirits, Williams from the outset sought a poetic Americanism. In effect, as he explains in the beautiful essays of *In the American Grain* (1925), America is not a given

13

reality but something we all make together with our hands, our eyes, our brains, and our lips. The American reality is material, mental, visual, and above all, verbal: whether he speaks Spanish, English, Portuguese, or French, American man speaks a language different from the European original. More than just a reality we discover or make, America is a reality we speak.

William Carlos Williams was born in Rutherford, New Jersey, in 1883. His father was English, his mother Puerto Rican. He studied medicine at the University of Pennsylvania. There he met Pound—a friendship that was to last throughout his life—and the poet H. D. (Hilda Doolittle), who fascinated the two young poets. After taking his doctorate and a short period of pediatric study in Leipzig, in 1910 he settled definitively in Rutherford. Two years later he married Florence Herman: a marriage that lasted a lifetime. Also for a lifetime he practiced a double vocation: medicine and poetry. Though he lived in the provinces, he was not a provincial: he was immersed in the artistic and intellectual currents of our century, traveled on various occasions to Europe, and befriended English, French, and Latin American writers. His literary friendships and enmities were varied and intense: Pound, Marianne Moore, Wallace Stevens, Eliot (whom he admired and condemned), e. e. cummings, and others, younger, like James Laughlin and Louis Zukofsky. His influence and friendship were decisive on Allen Ginsberg and also on the poetry of Robert Creeley, Robert Duncan, and the English poet Charles Tomlinson. (Poetic justice: a young English poet—and very English—praised by one who practiced almost his whole life a kind of poetic anti-Anglicism and who never tired of saying that the American language wasn't really English.) In 1951 he suffered his first attack of paralysis but survived a dozen years, dedicated to a literary program of rare fecundity: books of poetry, a translation of Quevedo, memoirs, lectures, and readings of his poems across the whole country. He died on 4 March 1963, where he was born and spent his life: in Rutherford.

His work is vast and varied: poetry, fiction, essays, theater, autobiography. The poetry has been collected in four volumes: *Collected Earlier Poems* (1906–1939), *Collected Later Poems* (1940–1946), *Pictures from Breughel* (1950–1962), and *Paterson* (1946–1958), a long poem in five books. Also there is a slim book of prose-poems which sometimes make one think of the automatic writing Breton and Soupault were engaged in around this time: *Kora in Hell* (1920). But in taking over a poetic form invented by French poetry, Williams changes it and converts it into a method of exploring language and the varied strata of the collective unconscious. *Kora in Hell* is a book which could only have been written by an American poet and ought to be read from the perspective of a later book which is the axis of Williams's Americanism, his *ars poetica*: *In the American Grain*. I will not consider his novels, stories, or theater pieces. Suffice it to say that they are extensions and irradiations of his poetry. The boundary between prose and verse, always hard to draw, becomes very tenuous in this poet: his free verse is very close to prose, not as written but as spoken, the everyday language; and his prose is always rhythmic, like a coast bathed by poetic surf—not verse but the verbal flux and reflux that gives rise to verse.

From the time he started writing, Williams evinced a distrust of ideas. It was a reaction against the symbolist aesthetic shared by the majority of poets at that time (remember López Velarde) and in which, in his case, American pragmatism was combined with his medical profession. In a famous poem he defines his search: "To compose: not ideas but in things." But things are always beyond, on the other side: the "thing itself" is untouchable. Thus Williams's point of departure is not things but sensation. And yet sensation in turn is formless and instantaneous; one cannot build or do anything with pure sensations: that would result in chaos. Sensation is amphibious: at the same time it joins us to and divides us from things. It is the door through which we enter into things but also through which we come out of them and realize that we are not things. In order for sensation to accede to the objectivity of things it must itself be changed into a thing. The agent of change is language: the sensations are turned into verbal objects. A poem is a verbal object in which two contradictory properties are fused: the liveliness of the sensation and the objectivity of things.

Sensations are turned into verbal objects by the operation of a force which for Williams is not essentially distinct from electricity, steam, or gas: imagination. In some reflections written down in 1923 (included among the poems in the late edition of *Spring and All* as "dislocated prose"), Williams says that the imagination is "a creative force which makes objects." The poem is not a double of the sensation or of the thing. Imagination does not represent: it produces. Its products are poems, objects which were not real before. The poetic imagination produces poems, pictures, and cathedrals as nature produces pines, clouds, and crocodiles. Williams wrings the neck of traditional aesthetics: art does not imitate nature: it imitates its creative processes. It does not copy its products but its modes of production. "Art is not a mirror to reflect nature but imagination competes with the compositions of nature. The poet becomes a nature and works like her." It is incredible that Spanish-language critics have not paused over the extraordinary similarity between these ideas and those that Vicente Huidobro proclaimed in statements and manifestos. True, it's a matter of ideas that appear in the work of many poets and artists of that time (for example, in Reverdy, who initiated Huidobro into modern poetry), but the similarity between the North American and Latin American are impressive. Both *invert* in almost the same terms the Aristotelian aesthetic and *convert* it for the modern era: imagination is, like electricity, a form of energy, and the poet is the transmitter.

The poetic theories of Williams and the "Creationism" of Huidobro are twins, but hostile twins. Huidobro sees in poetry something homologous with magic and, like a primitive shaman who *makes* rain, wants to make poetry; Williams conceives of poetic imagination as an activity that completes and rivals science. Nothing is further from magic than Williams. In a moment of childish egotism, Huidobro said: "The poet is a little God," an expression that the American poet would have rejected. Another difference: Huidobro tried to produce verbal objects which were not imitations of real objects and which even negated them. Art as a means of escaping reality. The title of one of his books is also a definition of his purpose: *Horizonte cuadrado (Square Horizon)*. Attempting the impossible: one need only compare the pictures of abstract painters with the images which microscopes and telescopes provide us to realize that we cannot get away from nature. For Williams the artist—it is significant that he was supported and inspired by the example of Juan Gris—*separates* the things of the imagination from the things of reality: cubist reality is not the table, the cup, the pipe, and the newspaper as they are but *another* reality, no less real. This *other* reality does not deny the reality of real things: it is *another* thing which is *the same thing* at the same time. "The mountain and the sea in a picture by Juan Gris," Williams says, "are not the mountain and the sea but a painting of the mountain and the sea." The poem-thing isn't the thing: it is something else which exchanges signs of intelligence with the thing.

The non-imitative realism of Williams brings him close to two other poets: Jorge Guillén and Francis Ponge. (Again, I am pointing out coincidences, not influences.) A line of Guillén's defines their common repugnance for symbols: "the little birds chirp without design of grace." Do design and grace disappear? No: they enter the poem surreptitiously, without the poet's noticing. The "design of grace" is no longer in the real birds but in the text. The poem-thing is as unattainable as the poem-idea of symbolist poetry. Words are things, but things which mean. We cannot do away with meaning without doing away with the signs, that is, with language itself. Moreover: we would have to do

17

away with the universe. All the things man touches are impregnated with meaning. Perceived by man, things exchange being for meaning: they are not, they mean. Even "having no meaning" is a way of meaning. The absurd is one of the extremes that meaning reaches when it examines its conscience and asks itself, What is the meaning of meaning? Ambivalence of meaning: it is the fissure through which we enter things and the fissure through which being escapes from them.

Meaning ceaselessly undermines the poem; it seeks to reduce its reality as an object of the senses and as a unique thing to an idea, a definition, or a "message." To protect the poem from the ravages of meaning, poets stress the material aspect of language. In poetry, the physical properties of the sign, audible and visible, are not less but more important than the semantic properties. Or rather: meaning returns to sound and becomes its servant. The poet works on the nostalgia which the signified feels for the signifier. In Ponge this process is achieved by the constant play between prose and poetry, fantastic humor and common sense. The result is a new being: the *objeu*. All the same, we can make fun of meaning, disperse and pulverize it, but we cannot annihilate it: whole or in living fragments and wriggling, like the slices of a serpent, meaning reappears. The creative description of the world turns, on the one hand, into a criticism of the world (Ponge as moralist); on the other, into *proeme* (the *précieux* Ponge, a sort of Gracián of objects). In Guillén the celebration of the world and of things results in history, satire, elegy: again, meaning. Williams's solution to the amphibious nature of language—words are things and are meanings—is different. He is not a European with a history behind him ready made but one ahead and to be made. He does not correct poetry with the morality of prose or convert humor into a teacher of resignation in song. On the contrary: prose is a ground where poetry grows, and humor is the spur of the imagination. Williams is a sower of poetic seeds.

The American language is a buried seed which can only come to fruition if irrigated and shone upon by poetic imagination. Partial reconciliation, always partial and provisional, between meaning and thing. Meaning—criticism of the world in Guillén, of language in Ponge—becomes in Williams an active power at the service of things. Meaning *makes*, is the midwife of objects. His art seeks "to reconcile people and stones through metaphor," American man and his landscape, speaking being with mute object. The poem is a metaphor in which objects speak and words cease to be ideas to become sensible objects. Eye and ear: the object heard and the word drawn. In connection with the first, Williams was the master and friend of the so-called Objectivists: Zukofsky, Oppen; in connection with the second, of the Black Mountain school: Olson, Duncan, Creeley. Imagination not only sees: it hears; not only hears: it says. In his search for the American language, Williams finds (hears) the basic measure, a meter of variable foot but with a triadic accentual base. "We know nothing," he says, "but the dance: the measure is all we know." The poem-thing is a verbal object, rhythmical. Its rhythm is a transmutation of the language of a people. By means of language Williams makes the leap from thing and sensation to the world of history.

Paterson is the result of these concerns. Williams goes from the poem-thing to the poem-as-system-of-things. Single and multiple system: single as a city were it one man only, multiple as a woman were she many flowers. *Paterson* is the biography of a city of the industrial East of the United States and the history of one man. City and man are fused in the image of a waterfall that cascades down, with a deafening roar, from the stone mouth of the mountain. Paterson has been founded at the foot of that mountain. The cataract is language itself, the people who never know what they say and who wander always in search of the meaning of what they say. Cataract and mountain, man and woman, poet and people, preindustrial and industrial age, the incoherent noise of the cascade and the search for a measure, a meaning. *Paterson* belongs to the poetic *genre* invented by modern American poetry which oscillates between the *Aeneid* and a treatise on political economy, the *Divine Comedy* and journalism: huge collections of fragments, the most imposing example of which is Pound's *Cantos*.

All these poems, obsessed as much by a desire to *speak* the American reality as to *make* it, are the contemporary descendants of Whitman, and all of them, one way or another, set out to fulfill the prophecy of *Leaves of Grass*. And in a sense they do fulfill it, but negatively. Whitman's theme is the embodiment of the future in America. Marriage of the concrete and the universal, present and future: American democracy is the universalizing of national-bound European man and his rerooting in a particular land and society. The particularity consists in the fact that that society and that place are not a tradition but a present fired toward the future. Pound, Williams, and even Hart Crane are the other side of this promise: their poems demonstrate to us the ruins of that project. Ruins no less grand and impressive than the others. Cathedrals are the ruins of Christian eternity, *stupas* are the ruins of Buddhist vacuity, the Greek temples of the *polis* and of geometry, but the big American cities and their suburbs are the living ruins of the future. In those huge industrial wastebins the philosophy and morality of progress have come to a standstill. With the modern world ends the titanism of the future, compared with which the titanisms of the past—Incas, Romans, Chinese, Egyptians—seem childish sand castles.

Williams's poem is complex and uneven. Beside magical or realistic fragments of great intensity, there are long disjointed chunks. Written in the face of and sometimes against *The Waste Land* and the *Cantos*, it gets out of hand in its polemic with these two works. This is its principal limitation: reading it depends on other readings, so that the reader's judgment turns fatally to comparison. The vision Pound and Eliot had of the modern world was somber. Their pessimism was instinct with feudal nostalgias and precapitalist concepts; thus their just condemnation of money and modernity turned immediately into conservative and, in Pound's case, Fascist attitudes. Though Williams's vision is not optimistic either—how could it be?—there are in it no reminiscences of other ages. This could be an advantage, but it is not: Williams has no philosophic or religious system, no coherent collection of ideas and beliefs. What his immediate tradition (Whitman) offered him was unusable. There is a kind of void at the center of Williams's conception (though not in his short poems) which is the very void of contemporary American culture. The Christianity of *The Waste Land* is a truth that has been burned, calcined, and which, in my view, will not put out leaves again, but it was a central truth which, like light from a dead star, still *touches* us. I find nothing like that in *Paterson*. Comparison with the *Cantos* is not to Williams's advantage either. The United States is an imperial power, and if Pound could not be its Virgil he was at least its Milton: his theme is the fall of a great power. The United States gained a world but lost its soul, its future—that universal future in which Whitman believed. Perhaps on account of his very integrity and morality, Williams did not see the imperial aspect of his country, its demonic dimension.

Paterson has neither the unity nor the religious authenticity of *The Waste Land*—even if Eliot's religious feeling is negative. The *Cantos*, for their part, are an incomparably vaster and richer poem than Williams's, one of the few contemporary texts that stand up to our terrible age. So what? The greatness of a poet is not measured by the extent but by the intensity and perfection of his works. Also by their liveliness. Williams is the author of the *liveliest* modern American poems. Yvor Winters rightly says, "Herrick is less great than Shakespeare but probably he is no less fine and will last as long as he. . . . Williams will be almost as indestructible as Herrick; at the end of this century we will see

21

him recognized, along with Wallace Stevens, as one of the two best poets of his generation." The prophecy came true before Winters expected it to. As to his ideas about New World poetry— is he really the most American of the poets of his age? I neither know nor care. On the other hand, I know he is the freshest, the most limpid. Fresh like a flow of drinking water, limpid as that same water in a glass jug on an unpolished wooden table in a whitewashed room in Nantucket. Wallace Stevens once called him "a sort of Diogenes of contemporary poetry." His lantern, burning in full daylight, is a little sun of his own light. The sun's double and its refutation: that lantern illuminates areas forbidden to natural light.

In the summer of 1970, at Churchill College, Cambridge, I translated six Williams poems. Later, on two escapades, one to Veracruz and another to Zihuatanejo, I translated others. Mine are not literal translations: literalness is not only impossible but reprehensible. Nor are they (I wish they were!) re-creations: they are approximations and, at times, transpositions. What I most regret is that I was unable to find in Spanish a rhythm equivalent to Williams's. But rather than embroil myself in the endless subject of poetry translation, I prefer to tell how I met him. Donald Allen sent me an English version of a poem of mine ("Hymn Among Ruins"). The translation impressed me for two reasons: it was magnificent, and its author was William Carlos Williams. I vowed that I would meet him, and on one of my trips to New York I asked Donald Allen to take me with him, as he had taken me before to meet cummings. One afternoon we visited him at his house in Rutherford. He was already half-paralyzed. The house was built of wood, as is common in the United States, and it was more a doctor's than a writer's house. I have never met a less affected man—the opposite of an oracle. He was possessed by poetry, not by his role as a poet. Wit, calmness, that not taking yourself seriously which Latin American writers so lack. In each

French, Italian, Spanish, and Latin American writer—especially if he is an atheist and revolutionary—a clergyman is concealed; among the Americans plainness, sympathy, and *democratic* humanity—in the true sense of this word—break the professional shell. It has always surprised me that in a world of relations as hard as that of the United States, cordiality constantly springs out like water from an unstanchable fountain. Maybe this has something to do with the religious origins of American democracy, which was a transposition of the religious community to the political sphere and of the closed space of the Church to the open space of the public square. Protestant religious democracy preceded political democracy. Among us democracy was antireligious in origin and from the outset tended not to strengthen society in the face of government, but government in the face of the Church.

Williams was less talkative than cummings, and his conversation induced you to love him rather than admire him. We talked of Mexico and of the United States. As is natural we fell into talking about roots. For us, I told him, the profusion of roots and pasts smothers us, but you are oppressed by the huge weight of the future which is crumbling away. He agreed and gave me a pamphlet which a young poet had just published with a preface written by him: it was *Howl* by Allen Ginsberg. I saw him again years later, shortly before his death. Though ill health had battered him hard, his temper and his brain were intact. We spoke again of the three or four or seven Americas: the red, the white, the black, the green, the purple. . . . Flossie, his wife, was with us. As we talked I thought of "Asphodel," his great love poem in age. Now, when I recall that conversation and write this, in my mind I pick the colorless flower and breathe its fragrance. "A strange scent," the poet says, "a *moral* scent." It is not really a scent at all, "except for the imagination." Isn't that the best definition of poetry: a language which does not say anything except to the imagination? In another poem too he says: "Saxifrage is my flower that splits open rocks." Imaginary flowers which work on reality, instant bridges between men and things. Thus the poet makes the world habitable.

Zihuatanejo, 20 January 1973

THE GRAPHICS OF
CHARLES TOMLINSON:
BLACK AND WHITE

When I first read one of Charles Tomlinson's poems, over ten years ago, I was struck by the powerful presence of an element which, later, I found in almost all his creative work, even in the most reflective and self-contemplating: the outer world, a presence at once constant and invisible. It is everywhere but we do not see it. If Tomlinson is a poet for whom "the outer world exists," it must be added that it does not exist for him as an independent reality, apart from us. In his poems the distinction between subject and object is attenuated until it becomes, rather than a frontier, a zone of interpenetration, giving precedence not to the subject but to the object: the world is not a representation of the subject—the subject is the projection of the world. In his poems, outer reality—more than merely the space in which our actions, thoughts, and emotions unfold—is a climate which involves us, an impalpable substance, at once physical and mental, which we penetrate and which penetrates us. The world turns to air, temperature, sensation, thought; and we become stone, window, orange peel, turf, oil stain, helix.

Against the idea of the world-as-spectacle, Tomlinson opposes the concept—a very English one—of the world as event. His poems are neither a painting nor a description of the object or its more or less constant properties; what interests him is the process which leads it to be the object that it is. He is fascinated—with his eyes open: a lucid fascination—at the universal busyness, the continuous generation and degeneration of things. His is a poetry of the minimal catastrophes and resurrections of which the great catastrophe and resurrection of the world is composed. Objects are unstable congregations ruled alternately by the forces of attraction and repulsion. Process and not transition: not the place of departure and the place of arrival but what we are when we depart and what we have become when we arrive. . . . The water-drops on a bench wet with rain, crowded on the edge of a slat, after an instant of ripening—analogous in the affairs of men to the moment of doubt which precedes major decisions—fall on to the concrete; "dropped seeds of now becoming then." A moral and physical evocation of the water-drops. . . .

Thanks to a double process, at once visual and intellectual, the product of many patient hours of concentrated passivity and of a moment of decision, Tomlinson can isolate the object, observe it, leap suddenly inside it, and, before it dissolves, take the snapshot. The poem is the perception of the change, a perception which includes the poet: he changes with the changes of the object and perceives himself in the perception of those changes. The leap into the object is a leap into himself. The mind is a photographic darkroom; there the images—"the gypsum's snow / the limestone stair / and boneyard landscape grow / into the identity of flesh" ("The Cavern"). It is not, of course, a pantheistic claim of being everywhere and being everything. Tomlinson does not wish to be the heart and soul of the universe. He does not seek the "thing in itself" or the "thing in myself" but rather things in that moment of indecision when they are on the point of generation or degeneration. The moment they appear or disappear before us, before they form as objects in our minds or resolve in our forgetfulness. . . . Tomlinson quotes a passage from Kafka which defines his purpose admirably: "to catch a glimpse of things as they may have been before they show themselves to me."

His procedure approaches, at one extreme, science: maximum objectivity and purification, though not suppression, of the subject. On the other hand, nothing is further from modern scientism. This is not because of the aestheticism for which he is at times reproached, but because his poems are experiences and not experiments. Aestheticism is an affectation, contortion, preciosity, and in Tomlinson we find rigor, precision, economy, subtlety. The experiments of modern science are carried out on segments of reality, while experiences implicitly postulate that the grain of sand is a world and each fragment figures the whole; the archetype of experiments is the quantitative model of mathematics, while in experience a qualitative element appears which up to now has been rebel to measurement. A contemporary mathematician, René Thom, describes the situation precisely and gracefully: "A la fin du XVIIième siècle, la controverse faisait rage entre tenants de physique de Descartes et de Newton. Descartes, avec ses tourbillons, ses atomes crochus, etc., expliquait tout et ne calculait rien; Newton, avec la loi de gravitation en l/r^2, calculait tout et n'expliquait rien." And he adds, "Le point de vue newtonien se justifie pleinement par son efficacité . . . mais les esprits soucieux de compréhension n'auront jamais, au regard des théories qualitatives et descriptives, l'attitude méprisant du scientisme quantitatif." It is even less justifiable to undervalue the poets, who offer us not theories but experiences.

In many of his poems, Tomlinson presents us with the changes in the particle of dust, the outlines of the stain spreading on the

27

rag, the way the pollen's flying mechanism works, the structure of the whirlwind. The experience fulfills a need of the human spirit: to imagine what we cannot see, give ideas a form the senses can respond to, *see* ideas. In this sense the poet's experiences are not less truthful than the experiments carried out in our laboratories, though their truth is on another level from scientific truth. Geometry translates the abstract relationships between bodies into forms which are visible archetypes: thus it is the frontier between the qualitative and the quantitative. But there is another frontier: that of art and poetry, which translates into sensible forms, that are at the same time archetypes, the qualitative relationships between things and men. Poetry—imagination and sensibility made language—is a crystallizing agent of phenomena. Tomlinson's poems are crystals, produced by the combined action of his sensibility and his imaginative and verbal powers—crystals sometimes transparent, sometimes rainbow-colored, not all perfect, but all poems that we can look through. The act of looking becomes a destiny and a profession of faith: seeing is believing.

It is hardly surprising that a poet with these concerns should be attracted to painting. In general, the poet who turns to plastic work tries to express with shapes and colors those things he cannot say with words. The same is true of the painter who writes. Arp's poetry is a counterpointing of wit and fantasy set against the abstract elegance of his painting. In the case of Michaux, painting and drawing are essentially rhythmic incantations, signs beyond articulate language, visual magic. The expressionism of some of Tagore's ink drawings, with their violence, compensates us for the sticky sweetness of many of his melodies. To find one of Valéry's watercolors among the arguments and paradoxes of the *Cahiers* is like opening the window and finding that, outside, the sea, the sun, and the trees still exist. When I was considering Tomlinson, I called to mind these other artists, and I asked myself how this desire to paint came to manifest itself in a meditative temperament such as his—a poet whose main faculty of sense is his eyes, but eyes which think. Before I had a chance to ask him about this, I received, around 1970, a letter from him in which he told me he had sent me one of the *New Directions Anthologies*, which included reproductions of some of his drawings done in 1968. Later in 1970, during my stay in England, I was able to see other drawings from that same period—all of them in black and white, except for a few in sepia; studies of cow skulls, skeletons of birds, rats, and other creatures which he and his daughters had found in the countryside and on the Cornish beaches.

In Tomlinson's poetry, the perception of movement is exquisite and precise. Whether the poem is about rocks, plants, sand, insects, leaves, birds, or human beings, the true protagonist, the hero of each poem, is change. Tomlinson hears foliage grow. Such an acute perception of variations, at times almost imperceptible, in beings and things necessarily implies a vision of reality as a system of calls and replies. Beings and things, in changing, come in contact: change means relationship. In those Tomlinson drawings, the skulls of the birds, rats, and cows were isolated structures, placed in an abstract space, far from other objects, and even at a remove from themselves, fixed and immovable. Rather than a counterpointing of his poetic work, they seemed to me a contradiction. He missed out some of the features which attract me to his poetry: delicacy, wit, refinement of tones, energy, depth. How could he recover all these qualities without turning Tomlinson the painter into a servile disciple of Tomlinson the poet? The answer to this question is found in the work—drawings, collages, and *decalcomanía**—of recent years.

Tomlinson's painting vocation began, significantly, in a fas-

---

*"*Decalcomanía* without preconceived object or *decalcomanía* of desire: by means of a thick brush, spread out black gouache, more or less diluted in places, upon a sheet of glossy white paper, and cover at once with a second sheet, upon which exert an even pressure. Lift off the second sheet without haste"—Oscar Domínguez, quoted in *Surrealism* by Roger Cardinal and Robert Stuart Short.

cination with films. When he came down from Cambridge in 1948, he had not only seen "all the films"; he was also writing scripts which he sent to producers and which they, invariably, returned to him. This passion died out in time but left two enduring interests: the image in motion, and the idea of a literary text as support for the image. Both elements reappear in the poems and the collages. When the unions closed the doors of the film industry against him, Tomlinson dedicated himself energetically to painting. His first experiments, combining *frottage*, oil, and ink, date from that period. Between 1948 and 1950 he exhibited his work in London and Manchester. In 1951 he had the opportunity to live for a time in Italy. During that trip the urge to paint began to recede before the urge to write poetry. When he returned to England, he devoted himself more and more to writing, less and less to painting. In this first phase of his painting, the results were indecisive: *frottages* in the shadow of Max Ernst, studies of water and rocks more or less inspired by Cézanne, trees and foliage seen in Samuel Palmer rather than in the real world. Like other artists of his generation, he made the circuit round the various stations of modern art and paused, long enough to genuflect, before the geometric chapel of the Braques, the Légers, and the Grises. During those same years—getting on toward 1954—Tomlinson was writing the splendid *Seeing Is Believing* poems. He ceased painting.

The interruption was not long. Settled near Bristol, he returned to his brushes and crayons. The temptation to use black (why? he still asks himself) had an unfortunate effect: by exaggerating the contours, it made his compositions stiff. "I wanted to reveal the pressure of objects," he wrote to me, "but all I managed to do was thicken the outlines." In 1968 Tomlinson seriously confronted his vocation and the obstacles to it. I refer to his inner inhibitions and, most of all, to that mysterious predilection for black. As always happens, an intercessor appeared: Seghers. Tomlinson was wise to have chosen Hercules Seghers—each of us has the intercessors he deserves. It is worth noting that the work of this great artist—I am thinking of his impressive stony landscapes done in white, black, and sepia—also inspired Nicolas de Staël. Seghers's lesson is: Do not abandon black, do not resist it, but embrace it, walk around it as you walk around a mountain. Black was not an enemy but an accomplice. If it was not a bridge, then it was a tunnel: if he followed it to the end it would bring him through to the other side, to the light. Tomlinson had found the key which had seemed lost. With that key he unlocked the door so long bolted against him and entered a world which, despite its initial strangeness, he soon recognized as his own. In that world black ruled. It was not an obstacle but an ally. The ascetic black and white proved to be rich, and the limitation on the use of materials provoked the explosion of forms and fantasy.

In the earliest drawings of this period, Tomlinson began with the method which shortly afterward he was to use in his collages: he set the image in a literary context and thus built up a system of visual echoes and verbal correspondences. It was only natural that he should have selected one of Mallarmé's sonnets in which the sea snail is a spiral of resonances and reflections. The encounter with surrealism was inevitable—not to repeat the experiences of Ernst or Tanguy but to find the route back to himself. Perhaps it would be best to quote a paragraph of the letter I mentioned before: "Why couldn't I make their world my world? But in my own terms. In poetry I had always been drawn to impersonality—how could I go beyond the self in painting?" Or put another way: how to use the surrrealists' psychic automatism without lapsing into subjectivism? In poetry we accept the accident and use it even in the most conscious and premeditated works. Rhyme, for example, is an accident; it appears unsummoned, but, as soon as we accept it, it turns into a choice and a rule. Tomlinson asked himself: what in painting is the equivalent

31

of rhyme in poetry? What is *given* in the visual arts? Oscar Dom-
ínguez answered that question with his *decalcomanía*. In fact,
Domínguez was a bridge to an artist closer to Tomlinson's own
sensibility. In those days he was obsessed by Gaudí, and by the
memory of the dining-room windows in Casa Batlló. He drew
them many times: what would happen if we could look out from
these windows on the lunar landscape?

Those two impulses, Domínguez's *decalcomanía* and Gaudí's
architectural arabesques, fused: "Then, I conceived of the idea
of cutting and contrasting sections of a sheet of *decalcomanía*
and fitting them into the irregular windowpanes. . . . Scissors!
Here was the instrument of choice. I found I could *draw* with
scissors, reacting *with* and *against* the *decalcomanía*. . . . Finally
I took a piece of paper, cut out the shape of Gaudí's window
and moved this mask across my *decalcomanía* until I found my
moonscape. . . . The 18th of June 1970 was a day of discovery
for me: I made my best arabesque of a mask, fitted it round a
paint blot and then extended the idea of reflection implicit in the
blot with geometric lines. . . ." Tomlinson had found, with dif-
ferent means from those he used in his poetry but with analogous
results, a visual counterpoint for his verbal world: a counter-
pointing and a complement.

The quotes from Tomlinson's letter reveal with involuntary
but overwhelming clarity the double function of the images, be
they verbal or visual. Gaudí's windows, converted by Tomlinson
into masks, that is, into objects which *conceal*, serve him to *reveal*.
And what does he discover through those window-masks? Not
the real world: an imaginary landscape. What began on the 18th
of June 1970 was a fantastic morphology. A morphology and
not a mythology: the places and beings which Tomlinson's col-
lages evoke for us reveal no paradise or hell. Those skies and
those caverns are not inhabited by gods or devils; they are places
of the mind. To be more exact, they are places, beings, and things

revealed in the darkroom of the mind. They are the product of the confabulation—in the etymological sense of that word—of accident and imagination.

Has it all been the product of chance? But what is meant by that word? Chance is never produced by chance. Chance possesses a logic—is a logic. Because we have yet to discover the rules of something, we have no reason to doubt that there are rules. If we could outline a plan, however roughly, of its involved corridors of mirrors which ceaselessly knot and unknot themselves, we would know a little more of what really matters. We would know something, for instance, about the intervention of "chance" both in scientific discoveries and artistic creation and in history and our daily life. Of course, like all artists, Tomlinson knows something: we ought to accept chance as we accept the appearance of an unsummoned rhyme.

In general, we should stress the moral and philosophical aspect of the operation: in accepting chance, the artist transforms a thing of fate into free choice. Or it can be seen from another angle: rhyme guides the text but the text produces the rhyme. A modern superstition is that of art as transgression. The opposite seems to me more exact: art transforms disturbance into a new regularity. Topology can show us something: the appearance of the accident provokes, rather than the destruction of the system, a recombination of the structure which was destined to absorb it. The structure validates the disturbance, art canonizes the exception. Rhyme is not a rupture but a binding agent, a link in the chain, without which the continuity of the text would be broken. Rhymes convert the text into a succession of auditory equivalences, just as metaphors make the poem into a texture of semantic equivalences. Tomlinson's fantastic morphology is a world ruled by verbal and visual analogies.

What we call chance is nothing but the sudden revelation of relationships between things. Chance is an aspect of analogy. Its unexpected advent provokes the immediate response of analogy, which tends to integrate the exception in a system of correspondences. Thanks to chance we discover that silence is milk, that the stone is composed of water and wind, that ink has wings and a beak. Between the grain of corn and the lion we sense no relationship at all, until we reflect that both serve the same lord: the sun. The spectrum of relationships and affinities between things is extensive, from the interpenetration of one object with another—"the sea's edge is neither sand nor water," the poem says—to the literary comparisons linked by the word *like*. Contrary to surrealist practice, Tomlinson does not juxtapose contradictory realities in order to produce a mental explosion. His method is more subtle. And his intention is distinct from theirs: he does not wish to alter reality but to achieve a modus vivendi with it. He is not certain that the function of imagination is to transform reality; he is certain, on the other hand, that it can make it more real. Imagination imparts a little more reality to our lives.

Spurred on by fantasy and reined in by reflection, Tomlinson's work submits to the double requirements of imagination and perception: one demands freedom and the other precision. His attempt seems to propose for itself two contradictory objectives: the saving of appearances, and their destruction. The purpose is not contradictory because what it is really about is the rediscovery—more precisely, the re-living—of the original act of making. The experience of art is one of the experiences of Beginning: that archetypal moment in which, combining one set of things with another to produce a new, we reproduce the very moment of the making of the worlds. Intercommunication between the letter and the image, the *decalcomanía* and the scissors, the window and the mask, those things which are hard-looking and those which are soft-looking, the photograph and the drawing, the hand and the compass, the reality which we see with our eyes and the reality which closes our eyes so that we see it: the search for a lost identity. Or as Tomlinson puts it best: "to reconcile the I that is with the I that I am." In the nameless, impersonal I that is are fused the I that measures and the I that dreams, the I that thinks and the I that breathes, the I which creates and the I which destroys.

Cambridge, Massachusetts, 1975

Jean-Paul Sartre:
A Memento

The death of Jean-Paul Sartre, after the initial shock this kind of news produces, aroused in me a feeling of resigned melancholy. I lived in Paris in the postwar years, which were the high noon of his glory and influence. Sartre bore that celebrity with humor and simplicity; despite the bigotry of many of his admirers which was irritating and funny at the same time, his simplicity, which was genuinely philosophical, disarmed more reticent spirits. During those years I read him with furious passion: one of his qualities was the way he could elicit from his readers, with the same violence, rejection and assent. Often, as I read, I lamented that I did not know him personally, so I might tell him face to face my doubts and disagreements. A chance incident gave me that opportunity.

A friend, sent to Paris by the University of Mexico to finish

Party, "the vanguard of the proletariat," and the ardent semi-anarchism of *The State and Revolution* there is an abyss. The figure of Lenin, like all human figures, is contradictory and dramatic: the author of *The State and Revolution* was also the founder of the Cheka and the forced-labor camps, and the man who initiated the dictatorship of the Central Committee over the Party.

Would Lenin, had he survived longer, have accomplished the democratic reform of both the Party and the regime itself? We cannot know. In his so-called Will he suggested that, to avoid a bureaucratic dictatorship, the number of members of the Central Committee of the Politburo should be increased. Rather like applying a poultice to cure a cancer. The evil was not (and is not) only in the dictatorship by the Committee over the Party but of the Party over the country. In any case, Lenin's suggestion was not taken up: the Politburo of 1974 is composed, like that of 1918, of eleven members, over which a Secretary General reigns. Nor did the other Bolshevik leaders reveal an understanding of the political problem, and all of them confused in a common scorn what they called "bourgeois democracy" and human liberty. Thanks perhaps to the influence of Bukharin, Lenin adopted a political program called NEP, which saved Russia from the great economic crisis which followed the civil war. But neither Lenin nor Bukharin thought of applying the NEP's economic liberalism to political life. Let's listen to Bukharin: "Among us too other parties can exist. But here—and this is the fundamental principle that distinguishes us from the West—the only conceivable situation is this: one party rules, the others are in prison" (*Troud*, 13 November 1927). This statement is not exceptional. In 1921 Lenin said, "The place for the Mensheviks and Revolutionary Socialists, both those who admit to it and those who conceal it, is prison. . . ." And to clear up any confusion between the economic liberalism of the NEP and political liberalism, Lenin writes to Kamenev in a letter dated 3 November 1922: "It is a big mistake to believe that the NEP has put an end to terror. We will have recourse to terror again and also to economic terror."

The majority of historians believe that the road which led to the Stalinist perversion began with the change from the dictatorship of the Soviets (councils of workers, farmers, and soldiers) to the dictatorship of the Party. Nonetheless, some forget that the theoretical justification of that confusion between the organs of the working class and the Party constitutes the very marrow of Leninism. Without the Party, Lenin said, there is no proletarian revolution: "The history of all nations shows that, by its own efforts, the working class is not capable of evolving beyond a syndicalist conscience." Lenin turns the working class into a minor, and makes the Party the true agent of history. In 1904, Trotsky commanded these ideas and anticipated the whole process, from the phase where the Party is above the proletariat to the phase in which the Central Committee is above the Party, and afterward to the phase in which the Politburo is above the Committee, until we reach the phase in which a dictator is above the Politburo.

Later Trotsky succumbed to the same aberration he had denounced. With his habitual clarity and coherence, in *Terrorism and Communism* (1920), he applied the Leninist ideas of the function of the "vanguard" of the Party:

> We have been accused more than once of substituting the Party dictatorship for the dictatorship of the Soviets. Nonetheless, we can affirm without risk of error that the dictatorship of the Soviets has not been possible without the dictatorship of the Party. . . . The substitution of the power of the working class by the power of the Party has not been a fortuitous or chance occurrence: the Communists express the fundamental interests of the working class. . . . But, some cunning critics ask, who guarantees that it is precisely *your* Party that expresses the historical evolution? In suppressing or repressing the other parties, you have eliminated political rivalry, the source of positive contention, and thus you have deprived yourselves of the possibility of verifying the soundness of the political line you have

adopted. . . . This critique is inspired by a purely liberal idea of the course of the revolution. . . . We have crushed the Mensheviks and the Revolutionary Socialists, and that judgment is enough for us. In any case our task is not to measure each moment, statistically, the importance of the groups that represent each tendency, but to make certain of the victory of our tendency, which is the tendency of the dictatorship of the proletariat. . . .

To justify the dictatorship of the Party over the Soviets, Trotsky substitutes the quantitative and objective criterion—that is, the democratic criterion which consists in "measuring" what tendencies represent the majority and what the minority—with a qualitative, subjective criterion: the supposed ability of the Party to interpret the "true" interests of the masses, even if against the opinion and will of these.

In the last great political debate within the Bolshevik Party which ended with the destruction of the so-called Workers' Opposition (Tenth Party Congress, 1921), Trotsky said:

The Workers' Opposition has made fetishes of democratic principles. It has placed the right of the workers to elect their representatives above Party, to put it in those terms, as though the Party hadn't the right to impose its dictatorship, even if that dictatorship were temporarily to oppose the changing tendencies of workers' democracy. We must remember the historical revolutionary mission of the Party. The Party is obliged to maintain its dictatorship without bearing in mind the ephemeral fluctuations of spontaneous reactions among the masses and even the momentary vacillation of the working class. . . . The dictatorship does not rest at every moment on the formal principle of workers' democracy.

In his Will Lenin reproaches Trotsky for his arrogance ("he has too much confidence in himself") and his bureaucratic tendencies ("he is too much inclined not to consider any but the purely administrative side of things"). But Lenin did not remark that those tendencies of Trotsky's personality had been justified in and nourished by the same ideas as his own on the relationship between the Party and the working classes. The same can be said of the personal tendencies of Bukharin and Stalin: Leninism was their common theoretical and political foundation. I do not wish to compare two eminent but tragically and radically wrongheaded men, Bukharin and Trotsky, with a monster like Stalin. I only point out their common intellectual affiliation.

The Leninist notion of political power is inseparable from the notion of dictatorship; and this, in turn, is conducive to terror. Lenin was the creator of the Cheka, and the Bolsheviks of the historic period were the first to justify the execution of hostages, the mass deportations, and the liquidation of whole collectives. Before Stalin murdered the Bolsheviks, Lenin and Trotsky physically annihilated, by violent and lawless means, the other revolutionary parties, from the Mensheviks to the Anarchists and from the Revolutionary Socialists to the left-wing Communist opposition. Years later, in exile, Trotsky repented, though only in part, and conceded, in *The Betrayed Revolution* (1936), that the first thing that had to be done in Russia was to re-establish the legality of other revolutionary parties. Why only the *revolutionary* parties?

In Marxism there were authoritarian tendencies that had their origin in Hegel. Yet Marx never spoke of the dictatorship of a single party, but of something very different: temporary dictatorship of the proletariat in the period directly after the taking of power. Leninism introduced a new element: the notion of the revolutionary party, the vanguard of the proletariat, which implies in its name the course of society and history. The essence of Leninism is not in the generous ideas of *The State and Revolution*, which appears too in other socialist and anarchist authors, but in the concept of a party of professional revolutionaries which embodies the march of history. This party tends to turn itself inevitably into a caste, as soon as it conquers power. The history of the twentieth century has shown us time and again the inexorable transformation of revolutionary parties into pitiless bureaucracies. The phenomenon has repeated itself everywhere: dictatorship by the Communist Party of the society; dictatorship of the Central Committee over the Communist Party; dictatorship of the revolutionary Caesar over the Central Committee. The Caesar can be called Brezhnev, Mao, or Fidel: the process is the same.

The repressive Soviet system is an inverted image of the political system created by Lenin. The forced-labor camps, the police bureaucracy that administers them, the arrests without process of law, the judgments behind closed doors, the torture, the intimidation, the calumnies, the self-accusations and confessions, the general spying: all this is the consequence of the dictatorship of the sole Party and, within the Party of dictatorship, of one group and one man. The political pyramid that is the Communist system is reproduced in the inverted pyramid of their repressive system. In turn, the repression the Party exercises on the populace is reproduced in the heart of the Party itself: the elimination of external opposition is succeeded necessarily by the elimination of internal rivals and dissidents: the Bolsheviks followed the road of the Mensheviks, Anarchists, and Revolutionary Socialists. President Liu-Shao-Ch'i and his old enemy Marshal Lin Piao lie now together, mingled in the same historical opprobrium. Recourse to bloody purges and cultural revolutions is no accident: how else can the middle and upper echelons of Party directors be renewed, and how else could political disputes and rivalries be resolved? The suppression of internal democracy condemns the Party to violent periodic convulsions.

EVEN IF we think economic structures are governed by us, it is impossible to ignore the decisive function of ideologies in historical life. Though according to Marx and Engels ideologies are mere superstructures, the truth is that these "superstructures" often outlive the "structures." Christianity outlived the bureaucratic and imperial regime of Constantine, medieval feudalism, the absolute monarchies of the seventeenth century, and the national bourgeois democracies of the nineteenth. Buddhism has revealed even greater vitality. And what of Confucianism? It will probably survive Mao, as it has survived the Han, the Tang, and the Ming. And, deeper than ideologies, there is another realm scarcely affected by historical change: beliefs. Magic and astrology, to call on two well-worn examples, have survived Plato and Aristotle, Abelard and Saint Thomas, Kant and Hegel, Nietzsche and Freud. Thus, to explain the repressive Soviet system we have to bear in mind various levels or strata of social and historical reality. For Trotsky, Stalinism was above all a consequence of the social and economic backwardness of Russia: the economic structure determined it. For other critics, it was rather the result of Bolshevik ideology. Both explanations are, at the same time, exact and incomplete. It seems to me that another factor is no less important: the very history of Russia, its religious and political tradition, all that half-conscious, airy element of beliefs, feelings, and images that constitutes what earlier historians called the *genius* (the soul) of society.

There is a clear continuity between the despotism exercised by Peter and Catherine and that of Lenin and Trotsky, between the bloodthirsty paranoia of Ivan the Terrible and Stalin. Stalinism and czarist autocracy were born, grew, and fed upon Russian reality. The same must be said of the bureaucracy and the police system. Autocracy and bureaucracy are features which Russia probably inherited from Byzantium, along with Christianity and the great art. Other features in Russian society are Oriental, and others have their origin in Slavic paganism. The history of Russia is a strange mixture of sensuality and exalted spiritualism, brutality and heroism, saintliness and abject superstition. Russian "primitivism" has been described or analyzed many times, now with admiration and now with horror. It is, one must confess, a very unprimitive primitivism: not only did it create one of the most profound, rich, and complex literatures in the world, but it also represents a living and unique spiritual tradition of our time. I am convinced that that tradition is called to give life, like a spring, to the drought, the egoism, and the decay of the contemporary West. The stories told by the survivors of the Nazi and the Soviet concentration camps reveal the difference between Western "modernity" and Russian "primitivism." In the case of the former, the words ceaselessly repeated are *inhumanity, impersonality,* and *homicidal efficiency*; while in the case of the latter, besides the horror and bestiality, words like *compassion, charity,* and *fraternity* stand out. The Russian nation has preserved, as one can see from the contemporary writers and intellectuals, a Christian foundation.

Russia is not primitive: it is *ancient.* Despite the Revolution, its modernity is incomplete: Russia did not have an eighteenth century. It would be useless to seek in its intellectual, philosophical, or moral tradition a Hume, a Kant, or a Diderot. This explains, at least in part, the coexistence in modern Russia of precapitalist virtues and vices such as indifference to political and social liberties. There is a similarity—as yet little explored—between the Spanish and the Russian traditions: neither they nor we, the Latin Americans, have a critical tradition because neither they nor we had in fact anything which can be compared with the Enlightenment and the intellectual movement of the eighteenth century in Europe. Nor did we have anything to compare with the Protestant Reformation, that great seedbed of liberties and democracy in the modern world. Thence the failure of the tentative democracies in Spain and its old colonies. The Spanish empire disintegrated and with it our countries too. Confronted with the anarchy which followed the dissolution of the Spanish order, we had no remedy but the barbaric remedy of tyranny. The sad contemporary reality is the result of the failure of our wars of independence: we were unable to rebuild, on modern principles, the Spanish order. Dismembered, each part became a victim of the chiefs of armed groups—our generals and presidents—and of imperialism, especially that of the United States. With independence, our countries did not begin a new phase: rather, the end of the Spanish world was hastened and achieved. When will we recover? In Russia there was no disintegration: the Communist bureaucracy replaced the czarist autocracy.

Like a good Russian, Solzhenitsyn would resign himself—he has said recently—to seeing his country ruled by a nondemocratic regime so long as it corresponded, however distantly, with the image that traditional thought created of the Christian sovereign, afraid of God and loving his subjects. An idea, I mention in passing, that has its equivalent in the "universal sovereign" of Buddhism (Asoka is the great example) and in the Confucian idea that the emperor rules by heavenly mandate. The Russian novelist's idea may seem fantastic, and to a certain degree it is. Nonetheless, it corresponds rather to a more realistic and deeper vision of the history of his country. And we, Spanish-Americans and Spaniards, is it not time that we examined more soberly and realistically our present and our past? When will we evolve our own political thought? A century and a half of petty tyrants, pronouncements, and military dictatorships—has this not opened our eyes? Our failure to adapt democratic institutions, in their two modern versions—the Anglo-Saxon and the French—ought to compel us to think on our own account, without looking through the spectacles of modish ideology. The contradiction between our institutions and what we really are is scandalous and would be comical were it not tragic. I feel no nostalgia for the Indian King or the Viceroy, for the Lady Serpent or the Grand Inquisitor, nor for His Most Serene Highness, or the Hero of Peace or the Great Chief of the Revolution. But these grotesque, frightening titles denote realities, and those realities are more real than our laws and constitutions. It is useless to close our eyes to them and more useless still to repress our past and condemn it to live on in history's subsoil; the life underground strengthens it, and periodically it reappears as a destructive eruption or explosion. This is the result of the ingenuity, hypocrisy, or stupidity of those who pretend to bury it alive. We need to *name* our past, to find political and juridical forms to integrate it and transform it into a creative force. Only thus will we begin to be free.

The system of sending delinquents against the common order along with political prisoners to Siberia was not a Communist but a czarist invention. The infamous Russian penal colonies were known throughout the world, and in 1886 an American explorer, George Kennan, devoted a book to this somber subject: *Siberia and the Exile System.* The reader need not be reminded of Dostoevski's *House of the Dead.* Less known is Anton Chekhov's *The Island, a Voyage to Sajalin.* But there is an essential difference: Dostoevski's and Chekhov's books were published legally in czarist Russia, while Solzhenitsyn had to publish his book abroad with the known risks. In 1890 Chekhov decided to travel to the celebrated penal colony of Sajalin and write a book on the Russian penitentiary system. Though it seems strange, the czarist authorities permitted his journey, and the Russian writer was able to interview the prisoners with considerable freedom (except for the political prisoners). Five years later, in 1895, he published his book, a complete condemnation of the Russian penal system. Chekhov's experience under czarism is unthinkable in any twentieth-century Marxist-Leninist regime.

As well as the circumstances of historical and national organizations, the place of individuals in the general order must be mentioned. Almost always these orders are interwoven with international realities and the national context. For example, in the case of Yugoslavia, Tito, as well as being the head of the Communist Party, led the nationalist resistance first against the Nazis and afterward against Stalin's attempts at intervention. Yugoslav nationalism contributed to the regime's relaxation of the terrible burden of the Russian and Leninist tradition: Yugoslavia humanized itself. It would be an error to ignore the beneficent influence of Tito's personality in that revolution. In each of the Communist states the Caesar imposes his style on the regime. In the time of Stalin, the color of the system was the rabid yellow and green of rage; today it is gray like Brezhnev's conscience. In China the regime is no less oppressive than in Russia, but its customs are not brutal or glacial: no Ivan the Terrible but Huang Ti, the first emperor. There is a striking resemblance between Huang and Mao, as Etiemble pointed out (see *Plural* 29, February 1974). Both rivals of Confucius and both possessed by the same superhuman ambition: to make time itself—past, present, and future—a huge monument that repeats its features. Time becomes malleable, history is a docile substance which takes on the kind and terrible imprint of the president-emperor. The first Cultural Revolution was the burning of the Chinese classics, especially the books of Confucius, ordered by Huang Ti in 213 B.C. Local variations on a universal archetype: the Caesar of Havana makes use of dialectics much as the old Spanish landowners used the whip.

THE SIMILARITIES between the Stalinist and Nazi regimes make it right for us to describe them both as totalitarian. That is the point of view of Hannah Arendt, but also of a man like Andrei Sakharov, one of the fathers of the Russian H-bomb:

> Nazism survived for twelve years; Stalinism twice as long. Besides the various common features, there are differences between them. The hypocrisy and demagogy of Stalin were of a more subtle order, depending not on a frankly barbarous program like Hitler's but on a socialist ideology, a progressive,

scientific, and popular ideology which was a useful screen to deceive the working class, and to anesthetize the vigilance of the intellectuals and of rivals in the struggle for power. . . . Thanks to that "peculiarity" of Stalinism, the most terrible blows were delivered to the Soviet people and their most active, competent and honorable representatives. Between ten and fifteen million Soviet citizens, at least, have perished in the dungeons of the NKVD, martyred or executed, and in the camps for "Kulaks" and their families, camps "without right of correspondence" (those camps were the prototypes for the Nazi extermination camps), or dead of cold and hunger or exhausted by the inhuman labor in the glacial mines of Norilsk and Vorkuta, in the countless quarries and forest exploitations, in the construction of canals or, simply, from being transported in closed train cars or drowned in the "ships of death" on the Sea of Okhotsk, during the deportation of whole populations, the Tartars from Crimea, the Germans from the Volga, Calmuks and other groups from the Caucasus. (*La liberté intellectuelle en URSS et la Coexistence*, Paris, Gallimard, 1968)

The testimony of the celebrated Soviet economist Eugene Varga is no less impressive:

Though in Stalin's dungeons and concentration camps there were fewer cruel men and sadists than in Hitler's camps, it can be affirmed that no difference in principle existed between them. Many of those executioners are still at liberty and receive comfortable pensions. (*Testament*, 1964: Paris, Granet, 1970)

However terrible the testimony of Solzhenitsyn, Sakharov, Varga, and many others, it seems to me that a crucial distinction ought to be made: neither the pre-Stalin period (1918–1928) nor the post-Stalin period (1956–1974) can be compared with nazism. Therefore one must distinguish, as Hannah Arendt does, between totalitarian systems properly speaking (nazism and Stalinism) and

Communist bureaucratic dictatorships. Nevertheless it is clear that there is a causal relationship between Bolshevism and totalitarianism: without the dictatorship of the Party over the country and the Central Committee over the Party, Stalinism could not have developed. Trotsky thought the difference between communism and nazism consisted in the different organization of the economy: state property in the former and capitalist property in the latter. The truth is that, beyond the differences in the control of property, the two systems are similar in being bureaucratic dictatorships of one group which stands above class, society, and morality. The notion of a separate group is crucial. That group is a political party which initially takes the form of a gathering of conspirators. When it takes power, the conspirators' secret cell becomes the police cell, equally secret, for interrogation and torture. Leninism is not Stalinism but one of its antecedents. The others are in the Russian past, as well as in human nature.

Beyond Leninism is Marxism. I allude to the original Marxism, worked out by Marx and Engels in their mature years. That Marxism too contains the germs of authoritarianism—though to a far lesser degree than in Lenin and Trotsky—and many of the criticisms Bakunin leveled at it are still valid. But the germs of liberty which are found in the writings of Marx and Engels are no less fertile and powerful than the dogmatic Hegelian inheritance. And another thing: the socialist program is essentially a Promethean program of liberation of men and nations. Only from this point of view can (and ought) a criticism of the authoritarian tendencies in Marxism be made. In 1956 Bertrand Russell admirably summarized the stance of a free spirit confronting terrorist dogmas:

> My objections to modern Communism are far deeper than my
> objections to Marx. What I find particularly disastrous is the
> abandonment of democracy. A minority which leans for sup-
> port on the activities of the secret police must necessarily be-

come a cruel, oppressive and obscurantist minority. The dangers which irresponsible power engenders were generally recognized during the eighteenth and nineteenth centuries, but many, blinded by the external successes of the Soviet Union, have forgotten all that which was painfully learned during the years of absolute monarchy: victims of the curious illusion that they form part of the vanguard of progress, they have reverted to the worst periods of the Middle Ages. (*Portraits from Memory*, New York, 1956)

The rejection of Caesarism and of Communist dictatorship does not in any way imply a justification of American imperialism, of racism, or of the atomic bomb; nor a shutting of the eyes before the injustice of the capitalist system. We cannot justify what happens in the West and in Latin America by saying that what happens in Russia and Czechoslovakia is worse: horrors there do not justify horrors here. What happens among us is unjustifiable, whether it is the prison detention of Onetti, the murders in Chile, or the tortures in Brazil. But nor is it possible for us to be blind to the misfortunes of the Russian, Czech, Chinese, or Cuban dissidents. The defense of so-called formal liberties is, day by day, the first political duty of a writer, whether in Mexico, in Moscow, or in Montevideo. The "formal liberties" are not, of course, all liberty, and liberty itself is not the sole human aspiration: fraternity, justice, equality, and security are also desirable. But without those formal liberties—of thought, expression, of association and movement, of saying "no" to power—there is no fraternity, no justice, nor hope of equality.

On this we ought to be unswerving and denounce implacably all equivocations, confusions, and lies. It is inadmissible, for example, that people who even a few months ago were calling the freedom of the press a "bourgeois trick" and were encouraging students, in the name of a radicalism both hackneyed and obscurantist, to violate the principle of academic freedom now form committees and sign manifestos to defend that very freedom of the press in Uruguay and Chile. Recently Günter Grass was putting us on our guard, recalling the pseudoradical frivolity of German intellectuals in the period of the Weimar Republic. While there was democracy in Germany, they never ceased to scoff at it as an illusion and a bourgeois plot, but when, fatally, Hitler came, they fled—not to Moscow but to New York, doubtless to pursue there with increased ardor their critique of bourgeois society.

The moral and structural similarities between Stalinism and nazism should not make us forget their distinct ideological origins. Nazism was a narrowly nationalist and racist ideology, while Stalinism was a perversion of the great and beautiful socialist tradition. Leninism presents itself as a universal doctrine. It is impossible to be unmoved by the Lenin of *The State and Revolution*. Equally, it is impossible to forget that he was the founder of the Cheka and the man who unleashed terror against the Mensheviks and Revolutionary Socialists, his comrades in arms. Almost all Western and Latin American writers, at one point or another in our lives, sometimes because of generous but ignorant impulses, sometimes out of weakness under the pressure of the intellectual milieu, and sometimes simply to be modish, have allowed ourselves to be seduced by Leninism. When I consider Aragon, Eluard, Neruda, and other famous Stalinist writers and poets, I feel the gooseflesh that I get from reading certain passages in the *Inferno*. No doubt they began in good faith. How could they have shut their eyes to the horrors of capitalism and the disasters of imperialism in Asia, Africa, and our part of America? They experienced a generous surge of indignation and of solidarity with the victims. But insensibly, commitment by commitment, they saw themselves become tangled in a mesh of lies, falsehoods, deceits, and perjuries, until they lost their souls. They became, literally, soulless. This may seem exaggerated: Dante and his punishments for some wrongheaded political views? Who nowadays anyway believes in the soul? I will add that our opinions on this subject have not been mere errors or flaws in our faculty of judgment. They have been a sin in the old religious sense of that word: something that affects the whole being. Very few of us could look a Solzhenitsyn, or a Nadejda Mandelstam, in the eye. That sin has stained us and, fatally, has stained our writings as well. I say this with sadness, and with humility.

Mexico, March 1974

GULAG:
BETWEEN ISAIAH
AND JOB*

Some writers and journalists, in Mexico and elsewhere in America and Europe, have criticized with a certain harshness things—some of them admittedly far of the mark—that Solzhenitsyn has said in recent months. The tone of these recriminations, ranging from the vindictive to the relieved "I told you so," is that of the man who has had a weight lifted from his shoulders: "Ah, that explains it all, Solzhenitsyn is a reactionary. . . ." This attitude is another indication that the attacks against the revelations about the totalitarian Soviet system which the writer has made were

*This essay was published twenty months after Paz's first essay on Sol- zhenitsyn. It extends some of the arguments advanced in that piece and distinguishes between Solzhenitsyn the witness and Solzhenitsyn the social theorist.

accepted *à contre coeur* by many Western and Latin American intellectuals. It's hardly surprising: the Bolshevik myth, the faith in the essential purity and goodwill of the Soviet Union, above and beyond its failures and errors, is a superstition not easily eradicated. The ancient theological distinction between *substance* and *accident* continues to serve our century's believers with the same efficacy that it did in the Middle Ages: the substance is Marxism-Leninism and the accident is Stalinism. That's why, when Solzhenitsyn's early books were published, the brilliant, casuistical Lukács tried to turn their author into a "socialist realist," that is, a dissident *within* the Church. But Solzhenitsyn's emergence—not only his, but the appearance of many other independent Russian writers and intellectuals—was and is significant for precisely the opposite reason: they are dissidents outside the Church. Their repudiation of Marxism-Leninism is complete. This is what seems to me portentous: more than half a century after the October Revolution, many Russian spirits, perhaps the best—scientists, novelists, historians, poets, and philosophers— have ceased to be Marxists. A few have even returned—like Solzhenitsyn and Brodsky—to Christianity. It is a phenomenon incomprehensible to many European and American intellectuals. Incomprehensible and unacceptable.

I don't know if history repeats itself: I know that men change very little. There is no salvation outside the Church. If Solzhenitsyn is not a dissident revolutionary, he must be a reactionary imperialist. To condemn Solzhenitsyn, who dared to speak, is to absolve oneself—a self that has preserved its silence for years and years. The truth is that Solzhenitsyn is neither a revolutionary nor a reactionary: his is another tradition. When he repudiated Marxism-Leninism he repudiated too the "enlightened" and progressivist tradition of the West. He is as far from Kant and Robespierre as he is from Marx and Lenin. Nor does he feel drawn to Adam Smith or Jefferson. He is not liberal, not democrat, not capitalist. He believes in liberty—yes—because he believes in human dignity; he also believes in charity and comradeship, not in representative democracy nor in class solidarity. He would accept a Russia ruled by an autocrat, providing that autocrat were at the same time a genuine Christian: someone who believed in the sanctity of the human being, in the daily mystery of the other, who is our fellow creature. Here I ought to pause briefly to say that I disagree with Solzhenitsyn in this: Christians do not love their fellow creatures. And they do not love them because they have never *really* believed in otherness. History shows us how when they have found it they have converted it or destroyed it. At the root of Christians, as at the root of their descendants the Marxists, I perceive a terrible self-disgust which makes them hate and envy others, especially if those others are pagans. This is the psychological source of their missionary zeal and of the Inquisitions with which now one faction, now another, have darkened the planet.

Solzhenitsyn's Christianity is not dogmatic or inquisitorial. If his faith distances him from the political institutions created by the bourgeois revolution, it also makes him an enemy to the idolatry of Caesar and his embalmed corpse, and to the fanatic adherence to the letter of "holy writ," those two religions of Communist states. In short, Solzhenitsyn's world is a premodern society with its system of special laws, local liberties, and individual privileges of exemption. Yet, archaic though his political philosophy seems to us, his vision reflects with greater clarity than the critiques of his detractors the historical crossroads at which we find ourselves. I admit that often his line of reasoning fails to convince me and that his intellectual style is alien and contrary to my mental habits, my aesthetic tastes, and indeed my moral convictions. I am nearer to Celsius than to Saint Paul, I prefer Plotinus to Saint Augustine and Hume to Pascal. But Solzhenitsyn's direct and simple vision penetrates actuality and reveals to us what is hidden in the folds and creases of our days. Moral passion is a passion for truth and it provokes the appearance of truth. There is a prophetic element in his writings which I do not find in the work of any other of my contemporaries. Sometimes, as in Dante's tercets—though the Russian's prose is ponderous and his arguments prolix—I hear the voice of Isaiah and I recoil and rebel; at other times, I hear the voice of Job and I pity and accept. Like the prophets and like Dante, the Russian writer tells us of actuality from the other shore, that shore I dare not call eternal because I do not believe in eternity. Solzhenitsyn tells us what is happening, what is happening to us, what is violating us. He treats history from the double perspective of the now and the forever.

Apart from certain countries whose histories are separate from the general history of Europe toward the end of the seventeenth century (I'm thinking of Spain, Portugal, and the old American colonies of both nations), the West is living out the end of something which began at the close of the eighteenth century: that *modernity* which, in the political sphere, found expression in representative democracy, balance of power, the equality of citizens before the law, and the system of human rights and individual guarantees. As if it were an ironic and devilish confirmation of Marx's predictions—a confirmation in reverse—bourgeois democracy dies at the hands of its own historical creation. Thus Hegel's and his disciples' creative negation seems to fulfill itself in a perverse way: the infant matricide, destroyer of the old order, is not the universal proletariat but the new Leviathan, the bureaucratic state. Revolution destroys the bourgeoisie but not to liberate men—rather to enchain them more cruelly. The connection between the bureaucratic state and the industrial system, created by bourgeois democracy, is so close that a critique of the first implies necessarily a critique of the second.

MARXISM IS INADEQUATE IN OUR TIME because its critique of capitalism, far from including industrialism, includes an

131

apology for its works. To laud technology and believe in industry as the greatest liberating agent of man—a belief common to capitalists and Communists—was logical in 1850, legitimate in 1900, understandable in 1920, but it is scandalous in 1975. Today we are aware that the evil is implicit not solely in the system of ownership of the means of production, but in the means of production themselves. Naturally it is impossible to renounce industry; it's not impossible to stop making a god of it, or to limit its destructiveness. Apart from the noxious ecological consequences, perhaps irreparable, the industrial system includes social dangers which no one now can be blind to. It is inhuman and dehumanizes all that it touches, from the "lords of the machines" to their "servants," as the economist Perroux calls those involved in the process: owners, technocrats, and workers. Whatever the political regime in which it evolves, modern industry automatically generates impersonal structures of labor and human relations no less impersonal, pitiless, and mechanical. Those structures and those relations contain a power, like the germ of the future organism, the bureaucratic state with its administrators, its moralists, its judges and psychiatrists and camps for labor reeducation.

Ever since it first appeared, Marxism has pretended to know the secret of the laws of historical evolution. It has not, throughout its history, abandoned this pretense and it is found in the writings of all the sects into which it has split, from Bernstein to Kautsky and from Lenin to Mao. Nonetheless, among its prophecies for the future there is no mention of the possibility which now seems to us most threatening and imminent: bureaucratic totalitarianism as the unraveling of the crisis of bourgeois society. There is one exception: Leon Trotsky. I mention him—though one swallow doesn't make a summer—because his case is full of pathos. At the end of his life, in the last article he wrote, shortly before he was murdered, Trotsky evoked—without much faith in it, just in passing, as one who shakes off a nightmare—the hypothesis that the Marxist view of modern history as the final triumph of socialism might be a hideous error of perspective. Then he said that, in view of the absence of proletarian revolutions in the West, during the Second World War or immediately after it the crisis of capitalism would resolve itself in the appearance of totalitarian collectivist societies whose earliest historical realizations were, in those days (1939), Hitler's Germany and Stalin's Russia. Since then, some Trotskyite groups (though dissidents within that movement, like those that publish *Socialisme ou Barbarie*) have directed their analysis into the area indicated by Trotsky, but they have not managed to devise a genuinely Marxist theory of totalitarian collectivism. The main obstacle in the way of a clear understanding of the phenomenon is their failure to recognize, as their teacher had, the class nature of the bureaucracy.*

Oddly, the only thing Trotsky thought of to confront the new Leviathan was—to elaborate a minimal program of defense of the workers! It's revealing that, despite his extraordinary intelligence, he did not consider two circumstances. The first is that he, with his dogmatic intolerance and his rigid conception of the Bolshevik Party as the instrument of history, had contributed powerfully to the construction of the world's first bureaucratic state. That irony is the more wounding if we remember that Lenin, in his Will, reproaches Trotsky for his bureaucratic leanings and his tendency to treat problems from the purely administrative angle. The second circumstance is the disproportion between the magnitude of the evil Trotsky perceived—a totalitarian collectivism instead of socialism—and the inanity of the remedy: a minimal plan of action. A curious vision of professional revo-

---

*I was too sweeping. We owe to Cornelius Costariadis and to Claude Lefort valuable and illuminating analyses of the historical nature of the Russian bureaucratic State that vastly overcome the limitations of the traditional Trotskyite critique. See my book *One Earth, Four or Five Worlds* (1985).

lutionaries: they reduce the history of the world to the editing of a manifesto and the forming of committees. Bureaucracy and apocalypse.

The bureaucratic state is not exclusively found in countries called socialist. It happened in Germany and it could happen elsewhere: industrial society carries it in its womb. The great multinational companies prefigure it, as do other institutions that form a part of Western democracies, like the American CIA. Nonetheless, if liberty is to survive the bureaucratic state, it ought to find a different alternative to the ones that capitalist democracies offer today. The weakness of these democracies is not physical but spiritual. They are richer and more powerful than their totalitarian adversaries, but they do not know what to do with their power and their wealth. Without faith in anything beyond immediate profit, they have time and time again entered into pacts with crime. This is what Solzhenitsyn has said—though in the religious language of another age—and this is what has scandalized the Pharisees. I'll add something I should have said before: Western democracies have protected and continue to protect all the tyrants and petty tyrants of the five continents.

It's often said that Solzhenitsyn has revealed nothing new. That is true: we all knew that in the Soviet Union forced-labor camps existed and that they were extermination camps for millions of human beings. What is new is that the majority of "left-wing intellectuals" has at last accepted that the paradise was in fact hell. This return to reason, I fear, is due not so much to Solzhenitsyn's genius as to the salutary effects of Khrushchev's revelations. They believed as they were told and they ceased to believe as they were told. Perhaps for this reason few—very few— of them have had the humble courage to analyze in public what went wrong and to explain the reasons that moved them to think and act as they did. The reluctance to admit error is such that one of those hardened souls, a great poet, said: "How could I, a writer, have avoided erring, when History itself erred?" The Greeks and the Aztecs knew that their gods sinned, but modern men surpass the ancients: History, that fleshed-out idea, like a scatterbrained matron goes on a spree with the first comer, whether his name is Tamburlaine or Stalin. This is where Marxism has come to rest, a system of thought that presents itself as "the critique of heaven."

In an article I wrote on the publication of the first volume of *The Gulag Archipelago*, I emphasized that the respect Solzhenitsyn inspires in me does not imply adherence to his ideas or to his stance. I approve his criticism of the Soviet regime and of the hedonism, hypocrisy, and myopic opportunism of the Western democracies; I repudiate his simplistic idea of history as a battle between two empires and two trends. Solzhenitsyn has not understood that the century of the disintegration and liquidation of the European imperial system has also been the century of the rebirth of the old Asiatic nations, such as China, and the rise of young countries in Africa and elsewhere in the world. Will those movements resolve themselves in a gigantic historical failure like the failure, up to now, of Brazil and the Spanish American nations, born a century and a half ago out of the Spanish and Portuguese disintegration? It is impossible to know, but the case of China seems to point in the other direction.

Solzhenitsyn's ignorance is serious because its true name is arrogance. It is, above all, a very Russian trait, as anyone who has had dealings with writers and intellectuals from that country, whether dissident or orthodox, knows. This is another of the great Russian mysteries, as all readers of Dostoevski know: in Russians arrogance goes hand in hand with humility, brutality with piety, fanaticism with the greatest spiritual liberty. The insensibility and blindness of a great writer and a great heart: Solzhenitsyn the brave and the pious has revealed a certain *imperial* indifference, in the ample sense of the word, in the face of the sufferings of peoples humiliated and subjected by the West.

135

The strangest thing of all is that, being as he is a friend and witness to liberty, he should not have felt sympathy with the struggles of those peoples for freedom.

THE CASE OF VIETNAM illustrates Solzhenitsyn's limitations. His and his critics'. Those groups who opposed, almost always with good and legitimate reasons, the American intervention in Indochina denied at the same time something undeniable: the conflict was an episode in the battle between Washington and Moscow. Not to see it—or to try not to see it—was to be blind to what Solzhenitsyn and (also) Mao saw: the defeat of the Americans encourages the aspirations toward Soviet hegemony in Asia and Eastern Europe. Those same groups—socialists, libertarians, democrats, anti-imperialist liberals—denounced justifiably the immorality and corruption of the South Vietnamese regime but did not say a single word about the actual nature of the one that ruled in North Vietnam. A witness beyond suspicion, Jean Lacouture, has called the Hanoi government the most Stalinist in the Communist world. Its leader, Ho Chi Minh, directed a bloody purge against Trotskyites and other dissidents of the left when he took power. The cruel measures adopted by the triumvirate which rules Cambodia have shocked and shamed Western supporters of the Khmer Rouge. All this proves that the left is snared in its own ideology; that is why it has not yet found the means of combating imperialism without succoring totalitarianism instead. But Solzhenitsyn himself is a victim of the ideological snare: he said that the war in Indochina was an imperial conflict, but he did not say that it was also—and above all else—a war of national liberation. This was what legitimized it. To ignore this fact is to ignore not only the complexity of all historical reality but also its human and moral dimension. Manichaeism is the moralist's trap.

Solzhenitsyn's opinions do not invalidate his testimony. *The*

Gulag Archipelago is neither a book of political philosophy nor a sociological treatise. Its theme is something else: human suffering in its two most extreme aspects, abjection and heroism. It is not the suffering which nature or destiny or the gods inflict, but which man inflicts on his fellow man. The theme is as ancient as human society, ancient as the primitive hordes and as Cain. It is a political, biological, psychological, philosophical, and religious theme: evil. No one has yet been able to tell us why evil exists in the world and why evil abides in man. Solzhenitsyn's work has two virtues, both great: first, it is the account of something lived and suffered; second, it constitutes a complete and horrifying encyclopedia of political horror in the twentieth century. The two volumes which have appeared so far are a geography and an anatomy of the *evil* of our era. That evil is not melancholy or despair or *taedium vitae* but sadism without an erotic element: crime socialized and submitted to the norms of mass production. A crime monotonous as an infinite multiplication exercise. What age and what civilization can offer a book to compare with Solzhenitsyn's or with the accounts of the survivors of the Nazi camps? Our civilization has touched the extreme of evil (Hitler, Stalin), and those books reveal it. This is the root of their greatness. The resistance which Solzhenitsyn's books have provoked is explicable: those books are the evocation of a reality whose very existence is the most thorough refutation, desolating and convincing, of several centuries of utopian thought, from Campanella to Fourier and from More to Marx. Moreover, they are a life study of a loathsome society but one in which millions of our contemporaries—among them countless writers, scientists, artists—have seen nothing less than the adorable features of the Best of Future Worlds. What do they say to themselves now, if they dare to speak to themselves, the authors of those exalted travelogues to the USSR (one of them was called *Return from the Future*), those enthusiastic poems and those impassioned reports about "the fatherland of socialism"?

The Gulag Archipelago takes the double form of a history and a catalogue. The history of the origin, development, and proliferation of a cancer which began as a *tactical* measure at a difficult stage in the struggle for power and which ended as a social *institution* in whose destructive function millions of human beings participated, some as victims and others as executioners, guards, and accomplices. The catalogue: an inventory of the gradations—gradations also in the scale of being—between bestiality and saintliness. In telling us of the birth, the development, and the transformation of the totalitarian cancer, Solzhenitsyn writes a chapter, perhaps the most terrible chapter, in the general history of the collective Cain; in telling us the cases he has witnessed and those which other eyewitnesses have told him—witnesses in the evangelical sense of the word—he gives us a vision of man. The history is social; the catalogue individual. The history is limited: social systems are born, evolve, and die; they're ephemeral. The catalogue is not historical: it relates not to the system but to the human condition. Abjection and its complement: the vision of Job on his dungheap has no term.

Mexico, December 1975

138

JOSÉ ORTEGA Y GASSET: THE WHY AND THE WHEREFORE*

I write these lines with enthusiasm and with fear. Enthusiasm because I always admired José Ortega y Gasset; fear because—apart from my personal inadequacies—I do not believe one can summarize or judge in an essay a literary and philosophical oeuvre as vast and varied as his. A philosophy which can be summarized in a phrase is not a philosophy but a religion. Or its counterfeit: ideology. Buddhism is the most intellectual and discursive of religions; all the same, a sutra condenses the entire doctrine in the monosyllable *a*, the particle of universal negation. Christianity, too, can be stated in one or two phrases, such as "Love

*This essay first appeared in a special issue of the Madrid daily paper *El País* dedicated to the memory of José Ortega y Gasset on the twenty-fifth anniversary of his death.

one another" or "My kingdom is not of this world." The same thing happens, at a lower level, with ideologies. For example: "Universal history is the history of the war of the classes" or, in the liberal camp, "Progress is the law of societies." The difference is that ideologies pretend to talk in the name of science. As Alain Besançon says: the religious man *knows that he believes* while the ideologue *believes that he knows* (Tertullian and Lenin). Maxims, tags, the sayings, and the articles of faith do not impoverish religion: they are seeds which grow and fruit in the heart of the faithful. Philosophy, by contrast, is nothing if not development, demonstration, and justification of an idea or an intuition. Without explication there is no philosophy. Nor, of course, criticism of the philosophical work.

To the difficulty of reducing to a few pages so rich and complex a body of thought as Ortega y Gasset's, one must add the actual character of his writings. He was a true essayist, perhaps the greatest in the Spanish language; that is, he was a master of a genre which does not allow the simplifications of synopsis. The essayist must be diverse, penetrating, acute, fresh, and he must master the difficult art of using three dots . . . He does not exhaust his theme, he neither compiles nor systematizes: he explores. If he succumbs to the temptation to be categorical, as Ortega y Gasset so often did, he should introduce into what he says a few drops of doubt, a reserve. The prose of the essay flows in a lively way, never in a straight line, but always equidistant from the two extremes which ceaselessly lie in wait for it: the treatise and the aphorism. Two forms of freezing.

Like a good essayist, Ortega y Gasset came back from each of his expeditions through unknown lands with unusual discoveries and trophies but without having charted a map of the new land. He did not colonize: he discovered. This is why I have never understood the complaint of those who say he left us no complete books (that is, treatises, systems). Can one not say the same of

Montaigne and of Thomas Browne, of Renan and of Carlyle? The essays of Schopenhauer are not inferior to his great philosophical work. The same thing happens, in our century, with Bertrand Russell. Wittgenstein himself, author of the most rigorous and geometrical book of philosophy of modern times, felt after writing it the need to write books more like the essay, acts of unsystematic reflection and meditation. It was fortunate that Ortega y Gasset did not succumb to the temptation of the treatise or the summa. His genius did not predispose him to define or to construct. He was neither a geometrician nor an architect. I see his works not as a collection of buildings but as a net of roads and navigable rivers. An oeuvre to be traveled through rather than resided in: he invites us not to stay but to move on.

He touched on an astonishing diversity of themes. More astonishing is how frequently those various subjects resolve themselves in genuine discoveries. Much of what he said is still worth remembering and discussing. I have already mentioned the extraordinary mobility of his thought: to read him is to walk briskly along difficult byways toward hardly glimpsed goals; sometimes one reaches the destination and sometimes one remains on the outskirts. No matter: what is important is the making of trails. But to read him is also to linger before this or that idea, to put the book aside and risk thinking on one's own account. His prose marshals verbs such as *incite, instigate, provoke, goad*. Some have reproached him for certain harshnesses and arrogances. Though I, too, lament those acrimonies, I understand that our countries— always drowsy, especially when they are possessed, as they now are, by violent agitations—need those goadings and stabs. Others criticize him because he did not know how to speak quietly. That is also true. I still ask myself how to resist raising one's voice in countries that are violent and lethargic? I add that his best writings, above and beyond the stimulus they give us, also give us illumination. They are something unusual in Spanish: exercises in clarity which are also attempts at clarification. That was one of his great gifts to Spanish prose: he showed that clarity was a form of intellectual cleanliness.

His essays on—I don't know whether to call it social psychology or history of the collective soul—the discrimination between ideas and beliefs or between the revolutionary and the traditional spirit, his reflections on the evolution of love in the West and on fashion, the feminine and the masculine, age and youth, vital and historical rhythms—make one think more of Montaigne than of Kant and more of Stendhal than of Freud. He was a philosopher with the gift to penetrate deeply into the human. This gift was not that of a professional psychologist but of the novelist and historian, who see men not as solitary entities or isolated cases but as parts of a world. For the novelist and historian every man is already a society in himself. Though we are in Ortega y Gasset's debt for memorable essays on historical themes, it is sad that it never occurred to him, as it did to Hume, to write a history of his country. *Invertebrate Spain* would have been an admirable and memorable beginning for it: why did he not continue? It is also revealing that he did not use his powers of psychological divining to see himself. He was not an introvert and I do not imagine him writing a diary. There is something that I miss in his work: confession. Especially oblique confession, in the manner of Sterne. Perhaps the passion he felt for his circumstances—his great discovery and the axis of his thought— kept him from seeing himself.

His idea of the "I" was historical. Not the "I" of the contemplative, who has shut the door on the world, but of the man in relationship—it would be more just to say, in combat—with things and with other men. The world, as he explained many times, is inseparable from the "I." The unity or nucleus of the human being is an indissoluble relationship: the "I" is time and space; or: society, history—action. Thus it is not odd that among his best essays there are some on historical and political themes, such as *The Revolt of the Masses, The Theme of Our Time, The End of Revolutions* (full of extraordinary prophecies of what is happening today, though clouded by a cyclic idea of history which did not let him see completely the *unique* character of the revolutionary myth), *Man the Technician*, and so many others. Ortega y Gasset had, like Tocqueville, the highly rational ability to see what was coming. His lucidity contrasts with the blindness of so many of our prophets. If one compares his essays on contemporary historical and political themes with those of Sartre, one immediately perceives that he was more lucid and penetrating than the French philosopher. He was less often wrong, was more consistent, and thus saved himself (and us) all those rectifications which mar the work of Sartre and which ended with the late *mea culpa* of his last days. Comparison with Bertrand Russell, too, is not disadvantageous to Ortega y Gasset: the history of his political opinions, without being entirely coherent, does not abound in the contradictions and pirouettes of Russell's, who went from one extreme to the other. One can approve or reprove his political ideas, but one cannot accuse him—as one can the others—of inconsistency.

I may have been unfaithful to the tenor of his work in speaking of his *thought*. One ought rather to say, his *thoughts*. The plural is justified not because his thinking lacks unity but because it deals with a coherence inimical to system and which cannot be reduced to a chain of reasons and propositions. Despite the variety of the matter he dealt with, he did not leave us a dispersed oeuvre. On the contrary. But his genius was not interested in the form of theory, in the proper sense of the word, nor in the form of demonstration. He sometimes used the word *meditation*. It is exact, but *essay* is more general. Better said: *essays*, because the genre does not admit the singular. Though the unity of these essays is, clearly, of an intellectual order, their root is vital and even, I dare say, aesthetic. There is a way of thinking, a *style*, which is Ortega y Gasset's alone. In this method of operation which combines intellectual rigor with the aesthetic necessity of personal expression lies the secret of his work's unity. Ortega y Gasset not only thought about this and that but also, from his earliest writings, decided that those thoughts, even those he took from his teachers and from the tradition, would bear his hallmark. To think was, for him, synonymous with expression. This was the opposite of Spinoza, who wanted to see his discourse, purged of impurities and accidents of the "I," as the verbal crystallization of mathematics, of the universal order. In this Ortega y Gasset was not far from the father of the essay, Montaigne. Many of Montaigne's ideas are drawn from antiquity and from some of his contemporaries, but his indisputable originality is not in the reading of Sextus Empiricus but in the way in which he lived and relived those ideas and how, in rethinking them, he changed them, made them his own and, thus, made them ours.

The number of ideas—what are called *ideas*—is not infinite. Philosophical speculation, for the last two and a half thousand years, has consisted of variations and combinations of concepts such as movement and identity, substance and change, being and entities, the one and the many, first principles and nothingness, etc. Naturally, those variations have been logically, vitally, and historically *necessary*. In the case of Ortega y Gasset this rethinking of the philosophical tradition and the thought of his age culminated in a question about the *why* and *how* of ideas. He inserted them into human life: thus they changed their nature, they were not essences which we contemplate in an unmoving heaven but instruments, weapons, mental objects which we use and live. Ideas are the forms of universal coexistence. He took the questioning of ideas further, to investigate what underlies and perhaps determines them: not the principle of sufficient reason but the domination of inarticulate beliefs. It is an hypothesis which, in another form, has reappeared in our days: the *beliefs* of Ortega y Gasset are, for Georges Dumézil, psychic structures, elemental in a society, present in its language and in its conception of the other world and of itself. The explanation for the immense influence Ortega y Gasset had on the intellectual life of our countries lies, no doubt, in this notion he had of ideas and concepts as *whys* and *hows*. They ceased to be entities beyond us and became vital spaces. His teaching consisted of showing us what ideas were for and how we could use them: not to know ourselves nor to contemplate essences but to open for ourselves a passage in our given circumstances, to converse with our world, with our past and with our kin.

Discourse with Ortega y Gasset was often a monologue. Many have regretted this, with some reason. Still, one must grant that that monologue taught us to think and made us talk, if not with ourselves, then with our Latin American history. He taught us that landscape is not a state of the soul and that we are not mere accidents of the landscape. The relationship between man and his environment is more complex than the antique relationship between subject and object. The environment is a "here" seen and lived from a "me"; that *from a me* is always a *from here*. The relation between one pole and another is, more than a dialogue, an interaction. Ideas are reactions, acts. This view, at once erotic and polemic of human destiny, does not open into any beyond. There is no transcendence beyond the act or the thought which, when it is carried out, is exhausted: then, under threat of extinction, one must begin again. Man is a being who continually makes and remakes himself. The great invention of man is men.

This is a Promethean and also a tragic view: if we are a perpetual self-creation, we are an eternal rebeginning. There is no rest: end and beginning are the same. And there is no human nature: man is not a given but something that makes and discovers itself. From the beginning of the beginning, cast out of himself and out of nature, he is a being in the air; all his creations— what we call culture and history—are nothing more than contrivances to keep him suspended in the air so that he will not fall back into the bestial inertia that preceded the beginning. History is our condition and our liberty: it is what we are in and what we make. Yet history does not consist of settled accounts, but of a suspension in the air, rootless, outside nature. I have always been staggered by this vision of man as a creature in permanent struggle against the laws of gravity. But it is a vision in which the other face of reality does not appear: history as an incessant production of ruins, man as fall and continual self-unmaking. I fear Ortega y Gasset's philosophy lacked the weight, the gravity, of death. There are two great absences in his work: Epictetus and Saint Augustine.

His intellectual endeavor found three outlets: his books, his teaching, and the *Revista de Occidente* with its publishing list. His influence left a deep mark on the cultural life of Spain and Latin America. For the first time, after a two-century eclipse, Spanish thought was heard and discussed in Latin American countries. Not only were our ways of thought and our funds of information renewed and changed; literature, the arts, and the sensibility of the age also show the marks of Ortega y Gasset and his circle. Between 1920 and 1935 in the enlightened classes, as they were called in the nineteenth century, a *style* predominated which came from the *Revista de Occidente*. I am sure that Ortega's thought will be discovered, and very soon, by younger Spanish generations. I cannot conceive a *healthy* Spanish culture without his presence. It will, of course, be a different Ortega y Gasset from the one we knew and read: each generation invents its authors. A more European Spain—such as the one currently on the drawing board—will feel greater affinity with the tradition which Ortega y Gasset represents, which is the tradition that has always looked toward Europe. But European culture is living through difficult years and cannot any longer be the fount of inspiration that it was at the outset of this century. Moreover, Spain is also American, as Valle-Inclán admirably saw, while Unamuno, Machado, and Ortega y Gasset himself were blind to it. Nor did the poets of the generation of 1927, though they discovered Neruda, feel or really understand Latin America. Thus the return to Ortega y Gasset will not be a matter of repeating but of amending him.

In this vast, rich, and diverse oeuvre I note three omissions. I have already mentioned two. The first is the look inward, introspection, which is always resolved in irony: he never saw himself and therefore, perhaps, did not know how to smile at his reflection in the mirror. Another is death, the undoing which is all doing. Ortega y Gasset's man is intrepid and his sign is Sagittarius; all the same, though he can look the sun in the face, he never looks at death. The third omission is the stars. In his mental heaven the lively and intelligent stars have vanished, the ideas and essences, the numbers turned light, the ardent spirits which enraptured Plotinus and Porphyry. His philosophy is of thought as action; to think is to do, build, make way, coexist: it is not to see or to contemplate. The work of Ortega y Gasset is a passionate thinking about this world, but from his world many other worlds are lacking, those which constitute the other world: death and nothing, reversals of life, history, and reason; the inner kingdom, that secret territory discovered by the Stoics and explored, before all others, by the Christian mystics; and the contemplation of essences or, as Sister Juana Inés de la Cruz put it, in the only truly philosophical poem in our language, "First Dream," the contemplation of the invisible from here,

> not only of all created things
> under the moon, but of those also
> which, intellectual, lucid, are Stars . . .

Perhaps it could be argued that Ortega y Gasset's thought frees us from worshiping such stars, that is, frees us from the net of metaphysics; ideas are not in any mental heaven: we have invented them with our thoughts. They are not the traces of universal order nor the image of cosmic harmony: they are uncertain lights which guide us on in darkness, signals we make to one another, bridges to cross to the other shore. But this is precisely what I miss in his work: there is no other shore, no other side. The *ratiovitalism* is a solipsism, a cul-de-sac. There is a point at which the Western and Eastern tradition, Plotinus and Nāgārjuna, Chuang-tzu and Schopenhauer, meet: the final end, the supreme good, is contemplation. Ortega y Gasset taught us that to think is to live and that thought separated from living soon ceases to be thought and becomes an idol. He was right, but he cut away the other half of life and thought. Living is also, and above all, to glimpse the other shore, to suspect that there is order, number, and proportion in all that is and that, as Edmund Spenser said, movement itself is an allegory of repose:

> That time when no more Change shall be,
> But stedfast rest of all things firmly stayd
> Upon the pillours of Eternity.
> —"Mutability Cantos"

Because of this, his reflections on history, politics, understanding, ideas, beliefs, love, are a knowledge—not a wisdom.

This essay—written without notes and confiding in my memory—is not an examination of Ortega y Gasset's ideas but of the impression they have left on me. Like so many other Latin Americans of my age, I had passionate recourse to his books during my adolescence and early adulthood. Those readings marked and shaped me. He guided my first steps, and to him I owe some of my first intellectual delights. To read him in those days was almost a physical pleasure, like swimming or walking in a wood. Then I drew back from him. I got to know other countries and I explored other worlds. At the end of the war I settled in Paris. In those days they held in Geneva some international conferences which achieved a certain notoriety. They consisted of a series of six public lectures, given by six European figures and followed, in each case, by discussions in small groups. In 1951 I was invited to participate in these discussions. I accepted: one of the six lecturers was Ortega y Gasset. On the day of his lecture I listened to him emotionally. Also angrily: beside me some provincial French and Swiss professors were making fun of his accent when he spoke in French. On leaving, they wanted to belittle him: I don't know why they were offended. The discussion next day began badly due to the malevolence of these same professors, though, fortunately, a generous and intelligent intervention by Merleau-Ponty put matters straight. I paid little attention to those petty disputes: I wanted to get near Ortega y Gasset and talk to him. At last I managed to do so and the next day I visited him in the Hôtel du Rhône. I saw him there twice. He met me in the bar: a large room with rustic wooden furnishings and a huge window looking out on the impetuous river. A strange sensation: one could see the raging and frothing water falling from a high floodgate, but, because of the thickness of the windowpanes, one could not hear it. I remembered the line from Baudelaire: *Tout pour l'oeil, rien pour les oreilles.*

Despite his love for the German world and its mists, Ortega y Gasset was, in physical and spiritual terms, a man of the Mediterranean. Not wolf nor pine: bull and olive. A vague similarity—stature, manners, coloring, eyes—with Picasso. He could have said with more authority than Rubén Darío: "here, beside the Roman sea / I speak my truth. . . ." I was surprised by the flickering of his bird-of-prey look, I am not sure whether eagle- or hawklike. I realized that, like tinder, he was easily fired, though the blaze did not last long. Enthusiasm and melancholy, according to Aristotle the contradictory extremes of the intellectual temperament. He struck me as proud without being disdainful, which is the best kind of pride. Also open and able to take an interest in his fellow creature. He greeted me openly, invited me to take a seat, and asked the waiter to serve us whiskeys. In answer to his questions, I told him I lived in Paris and that I wrote poems.

He shook his head reprovingly and reprehended me: clearly Latin Americans were incorrigible. Then he spoke with grace, openness, and intelligence (why did he never, in his writing, use the familiar tone?) of his age and of his looks (those of a bullfighter who has cut off his pigtail), of Argentinean women (nearer to Juno than to Pallas), of the United States (something might yet sprout there, though it is an excessively horizontal society), of Alfonso Reyes and his little Asiatic eyes (he knew little about Mexico and that seemed to him enough), of the death of Europe and its resurrection, of the bankruptcy of literature, again of age (he said something which would have shaken Plotinus: thinking is an erection and I still think), and of much else.

The conversation tended, at times, toward exposition; then, toward narrative: anecdotes and happenings. Ideas and examples: a master. I sensed that his love of ideas extended to his auditors; he watched me to see if I had understood him. Before him I existed not as an echo; rather, as a confirmation. I understood that all his writings were an extension of the spoken word and that this is the essential difference between the philosopher and the poet. The poem is a verbal object, and though it is made of signs (words), its ultimate reality unfolds beyond those signs: it is the presentation of a form; the discourse of the philosopher uses forms and signs, it is an invitation to realize ourselves (virtue, authenticity, stoic calmness, what have you). I left him with my brain boiling.

I saw him again the next afternoon. Roberto Vernengo, a bright young Argentinean who was his guide in Switzerland and who was well acquainted with German and French philosophy, was with him. We went for a walk in the city. Roberto left us, and Ortega and I walked for a while, returning to his hotel along the bank of the river. Now one could hear the roar of the water falling into the lake. The wind began to blow. He told me that the only activity possible in the modern world was thought ("Literature is dead, it's a store that's closed down, though they still haven't found this out in Paris") and that, to think, one needed to know Greek or, at least, German. He halted for a moment and interrupted his monologue, took me by the arm, and, with an intense look which still moves me, he said: "Learn German and start thinking. Forget the rest." I promised to obey him and accompanied him to the door of his hotel. The next day I took the train back to Paris.

I did not learn German. Nor did I forget "the rest." In this I did follow him, however: he always taught that it is not necessary to think, in itself, that all thought is thought toward or about "the rest." That "rest," whatever name we give it, is our circumstance. "The rest," for me, is history; that which is beyond history is called poetry. We are living an Ending, but ending is no less fascinating and worthy than beginning. Endings and beginnings resemble each other: at the outset, poetry and thought were united; then an act of rational violence divided them; today they tend, almost at random, to come together again. And his third piece of advice: "start thinking"? His books, when I was a young man, made me think. From then on I have tried to be faithful to that first lesson. I'm not too sure that I think now as I did at that time; but I do know that without his thought I could not, today, think at all.

Mexico, October 1980

LUIS BUÑUEL:
THREE PERSPECTIVES

I BUÑUEL THE POET

The release of *L'Age d'or* and *Un chien andalou* signals the first considered irruption of poetry into the art of cinematography. The marriage of the film image to the poetic image, creating a new reality, inevitably appeared scandalous and subversive—as indeed it was. The subversive nature of Buñuel's early films resides in the fact that, hardly touched by the hand of poetry, the insubstantial conventions (social, moral, or artistic) of which our reality is made fall away. And from those ruins rises a new truth, that of man and his desire. Buñuel shows us that a man with his hands tied can, by simply shutting his eyes, make the world jump. Those films are something more than a fierce attack on so-called reality; they are the revelation of another reality which contemporary civilization has humiliated. The man in *L'Age d'or* slumbers in each of us and waits only for a signal to awake: the signal of love. This film is one of the few attempts in modern art to reveal the terrible face of love at liberty.

A little later, Buñuel screened *Land Without Bread*, a documentary which of its genre is also a masterpiece. In this film Buñuel the poet withdraws; he is silent so that reality can speak for itself. If the subject of Buñuel's surrealist films is the struggle of man against a reality which smothers and mutilates him, the subject of *Land Without Bread* is the brutalizing victory of that same reality. Thus this documentary is the necessary complement to his earlier creations. It explains and justifies them. By different routes, Buñuel pursues his bloody battle with reality. Or rather, against it. His realism, like that of the best Spanish tradition— Goya, Quevedo, the picaresque novel, Valle-Inclán, Picasso— consists of a pitiless hand-to-hand combat with reality. Tackling it, he flays it. This is why his art bears no relation at all to the more or less tendentious, sentimental, or aesthetic descriptions of the writing that is commonly called realism. On the contrary, all his work tends to stimulate the release of something secret and precious, terrible and pure, hidden by our reality itself. Making use of dream and poetry or using the medium of film narrative, Buñuel the poet descends to the very depths of man, to his most radical and unexpressed intimacy.

After a silence of many years, Buñuel screens a new film: *Los Olvidados*. If one compares this film with those he made with Salvador Dali, what is surprising above all is the rigor with which Buñuel takes his first intuitions to their extreme limits. On the one hand, *Los Olvidados* represents a moment of artistic maturity; on the other, of greater and more total rage: the gate of dreams seems sealed forever; the only gate remaining open is the gate of blood. Without betraying the great experience of his youth, but conscious of how times have changed, that reality which he denounced in his earlier works has grown even more dense— Buñuel constructs a film in which the action is precise as a mechanism, hallucinatory as a dream, implacable as the silent encroachment of lava flow. The argument of *Los Olvidados*—delinquent childhood—has been extracted from penal archives. Its characters are our contemporaries and are of an age with our own children. But *Los Olvidados* is something more than a realist film. Dream, desire, horror, delirium, chance, the nocturnal part of life, also play their part. And the gravity of the reality it shows us is atrocious in such a way that in the end it appears impossible to us, unbearable. And it is: reality is *unbearable*; and that is why, because he cannot bear it, man kills and dies, loves and creates.

The strictest artistic economy governs *Los Olvidados*. Corresponding to this greater condensation is a more intense explosion. That is why it is a film without "stars"; that is why the "musical background" is so discreet and does not set out to usurp what music owes to the eyes in films; and finally, that is why it disdains local color. Turning its back on the temptation of the impressive Mexican landscape, the scenario is reduced to the sordid and insignificant desolation, but always implacable, of an urban setting. The physical and human space in which the drama unfolds could hardly be more closed: the life and death of some children delivered up to their own fate, between the four walls of abandonment. The city, with all that this word entails of human solidarity, is alien and strange. What we call civilization is for them nothing but a wall, a great No which closes the way. Those children are Mexicans, but they could be from some other country, could live in any suburb of another great city. In a sense they do not live in Mexico, or anywhere: they are the forgotten, the inhabitants of those wastelands which each modern city breeds on its outskirts. A world closed on itself, where all acts are reflexive and each step returns us to our point of departure. No one can get out of there, or out of himself, except by way of the long street of death. Fate, which opens doors in other worlds, here closes them.

In *Los Olvidados* the continuous presence of the hazard has a special meaning, which forbids us from confusing it with mere chance. The hazard which governs the action of the protagonists is presented as a necessity which, nonetheless, *could have been avoided*. (Why not give it its true name, then, as in tragedy: *destiny?*) The old fate is at work again, but deprived of its supernatural attributes: now we face a social and psychological fate. Or, to use the magical word of our time, the new intellectual fetish: an historical fate. It is not enough, however, for society, history, or circumstances to prove hostile to the protagonists; for the catastrophe to come about, it is necessary for those determinants to coincide with human will. Pedro struggles against chance, against his bad luck or his bad shadow, embodied in the Jaibo; when, cornered, he accepts and faces it, he changes fate into destiny. He dies, but he makes his death his own. The collision between human consciousness and external fate constitutes the essence of the tragic act. Buñuel has rediscovered this fundamental ambiguity: without human complicity, destiny is not fulfilled and tragedy is impossible. Fate wears the mask of liberty; chance, that of destiny.

Los Olvidados is not a documentary film. Nor is it a thesis, propagandistic, or moralizing film. Though no sermonizing blurs his admirable objectivity, it would be slanderous to suggest that this is an art film, in which all that counts are artistic values. Far from realism (social, psychological, and edifying) and from aestheticism, Buñuel's film finds its place in the tradition of a passionate and ferocious art, contained and raving, which claims as antecedents Goya and Posada, the graphic artists who have perhaps taken black humor furthest. Cold lava, volcanic ice. Despite the universality of his subject, the absence of local color, and the extreme bareness of his construction, *Los Olvidados* has an emphasis which there is no other word for but *racial* (in the sense in which fighting bulls have *casta*). The misery and abandonment can be met with anywhere in the world, but the bloodied passion with which they are described belongs to great Spanish art. We have already come across that half-witted blind man in the Spanish picaresque tradition. Those women, those drunks, those cretins, those murderers, those innocents, we have come across in Quevedo and Galdós, we have glimpsed them in Cervantes, Velázquez and Murillo have depicted them. Those sticks—the walking sticks of the blind—are the same which tap all down the history of Spanish theater. And the children, the forgotten ones, their mythology, their passive rebellion, their suicidal loyalty, their sweetness which flashes out, their tenderness full of exquisite ferocity, their impudent affirmation of themselves in and for death, their endless search for communion—even through crime—are not and cannot be anything but Mexican. Thus, in the crucial scene in the film—the "libation" scene—the subject of the mother is resolved in the common supper, the sacred feast. Perhaps unintentionally, Buñuel finds in the dream of his protagonists the archetypal images of the Mexican people: Coatlicue [Aztec goddess of death and fertility] and sacrifice. The subject of the mother, a Mexican obsession, is inexorably linked to the theme of fraternity, of friendship unto death. Both constitute the secret foundation of this film. The world of Los Olvidados is peopled by orphans, by loners who seek communion and who do not balk at blood to find it. The quest for the "other," for our likeness, is the other side of the search for the mother. Or the acceptance of her definitive absence: the knowledge that we are alone. Pedro, the Jaibo, and his companions thus reveal to us the ultimate nature of man, which perhaps consists in a permanent and constant state of orphandom.

Witness to our age, the moral value of Los Olvidados bears no relation at all to propaganda. Art, when it is free, is witness, conscience. Buñuel's work proves what creative talent and artistic conscience can do when nothing but their own liberty constrains or drives them.

Cannes, 4 April 1951

II BUÑUEL'S
PHILOSOPHICAL CINEMA

Some years ago I wrote about Buñuel. This is what I said:

Though all the arts, even the most abstract, have as their ultimate and general end to express and re-create man and his conflicts, each of them has particular means and techniques of enchantment and thus constitutes its own domain. Music is one thing, poetry another, cinema something else again. But sometimes an artist manages to transcend the limits of his art; then we engage a work which finds points of reference outside its world. Some of the films of Luis Buñuel—*L'Age d'or, Los Olvidados*—while they remain films, take us toward other boundaries of the spirit: some of Goya's engravings, a poem by Quevedo or Péret, a passage from Sade, an absurd character from Valle-Inclán, a page of Gómez de la Serna. . . . These films can be enjoyed and judged as film and at the same time as something which belongs to the wider and freer world of those works, precious among all others, which have as their object not only to reveal human reality to us but also to show us a way to transcend it. Despite the obstacles which the real world sets in the way of similar projects, Buñuel's attempt develops under the double arch of beauty and rebellion.

In *Nazarin*, with a style that flees from all complacency and rejects all suspect lyricism, Buñuel tells us the story of a quixotic priest, whose concept of Christianity soon sets him at odds with the Church, society, and the police. Nazarin belongs, like many of Galdós's characters, to the great tradition of Spanish madmen. Their madness consists of taking Christianity seriously and of trying to live in accordance with the Gospels. The man who refuses to admit to himself that what we call reality is reality and not just an atrocious caricature of the true reality, is mad. Like Don Quixote, who discerned his Dulcinea in a peasant girl, Nazarin perceives in the monstrous sketches of

Andra the whore and Ujo the hunchback the helpless image of
fallen men; and in the erotic delirium of Beatriz, an hysteric,
he perceives the disfigured face of divine love. In the course of
the film—in which scenes in the best and most terrible Buñuel
manner, now with more concentrated and therefore more ex-
plosive rage, abound—we witness the *cure* of the madman:
that is, his torture. Everyone rejects him: the powerful and self-
satisfied because they consider him a nuisance and, in the end,
dangerous; the victims and the persecuted because they need
another, more effective type of consolation. He is pursued not
only by the powers that be, but by social equivoque. If he
begs for alms, he is an unproductive person; if he seeks work,
he breaks the solidarity of the salaried. Even the sentiments of
the women who pursue him, reembodiments of Mary Mag-
dalen, turn out ambiguous in the end. In the jail where his
good works have landed him, he receives the final revelation:
his "goodness," quite as much as the "evil" of one of his
companions in punishment, a murderer and church-robber, are
equally useless in a world which worships efficiency as the
highest value.

Faithful to the tradition of the Spanish madman, from Cer-
vantes to Galdós, Buñuel's film tells the story of a disillusion-
ment. For Don Quixote, illusion was the chivalric spirit; for
Nazarin it is Christianity. But there is something more. As the
image of Christ fades in Nazarin's consciousness, another be-
gins to emerge: that of man. Buñuel makes us witness, by means
of a series of episodes that are exemplary in the good sense of
the word, a double process: the disappearance of the illusion
of divinity and the discovery of the reality of man. The super-
natural gives place to the marvelous: to human nature and its
powers. This revelation is embodied in two unforgettable mo-
ments: when Nazarin offers *otherworldly consolations* to the
dying lover and she replies, gripped by the image of her beloved,
with a phrase that is genuinely frightening: *no to heaven, yes
to Juan*; and at the end, when Nazarin rejects the alms of a

poor woman, only to accept them after a moment of doubt—
no longer as a gift but as a token of comradeship. Nazarin
the loner has ceased to be alone: he has lost God but he has
found men.

This little text appeared in a handout that accompanied the
showing of *Nazarin* at the Cannes Film Festival. It was feared,
rightly as it proved, that confusion would arise over the meaning
of the film, since it is not only a criticism of social reality but
also of the Christian religion. The risk of confusion, which all
works of art run, was greater in this instance because of the nature
of the novel which inspired Buñuel. Galdós's theme is the old
opposition between the Christianity of the Gospel and its eccle-
siastical and historical distortions. The hero of the book is a
rebellious and enlightened priest, a true Protestant: he abandons
the Church but stays with God. Buñuel's film sets out to show
the opposite: the disappearance of the figure of Christ from the
consciousness of a sincere and pure believer. In the scene of the
dying girl, which is a transposition of Sade's "Dialogue Between
a Priest and a Dying Man," the woman affirms the precious,
irrecoverable value of earthly love: if there is a heaven, it is here
and now, in the moment of the carnal embrace, not in a timeless,
bodiless beyond. In the prison scene, the sacrilegious bandit ap-
pears no less absurd a man than the enlightened priest. The crimes
of the former are as illusory as the holiness of the latter: if there
is no God, there is no sacrilege or holiness either.

Nazarin is not Buñuel's best film, but it is typical of the duality
that governs his work. On the one hand, ferocity and lyricism,
a world of dream and of blood which immediately calls to mind
two other great Spaniards: Quevedo and Goya. On the other,
the concentration of a style not at all baroque in character which
leads him to a kind of exasperated sobriety. The straight line,
not the surrealist arabesque. Rational rigor: each of his films,
from *L'Age d'or* to *Viridiana*, is unfolded as a *demonstration*.

The most violent and free imagination at the service of a syllogism honed sharp as a knife, irrefutable as a rock: Buñuel's logic is the implacable reason of the Marquis de Sade. This name clarifies the relationship between Buñuel and surrealism: without that movement he would have been a poet and a rebel anyway; thanks to it, he sharpened his weapons. Surrealism, which revealed Sade's thought to him, was not for Buñuel a school of rapture but of reason: his poetry, while it remained poetry, became criticism. In the closed cloister of criticism, rapture spread its wings and clawed its own breast with its nails. Bullring surrealism, but also critical surrealism: the bullfight as philosophical demonstration.

In a primary text of modern letters, *De la Litterature Considerée comme une Tauromachine (Of Literature Considered as an Art of Bullfighting)*, Michel Leiris points out that his fascination with bullfighting depends on the fusion between risk and style: the *diestro* (skilled matador)—the Spanish word is exact—should face the bull's charge without losing composure. True: good manners are indispensable for dying and for killing, at least if you believe, as I do, that these two biological acts are at the same time rites, ceremonies. In bullfighting, danger achieves the dignity of form, and form the veracity of death. The bullfighter locks himself into a form which opens out on the danger of dying. It is what in Spanish we call *temple* (temper): musical intrepidity and fine tuning, hardness and flexibility. The bullfight, like photography, is an exposure, and the style of Buñuel, by matched artistic and philosophical choice, is that of exposure. To expose is to expose oneself, risk oneself. It is also to externalize, to show and to demonstrate: to reveal. Buñuel's stories are an exposure: they reveal human realities as they submit them, as if they were photographic plates, to the light of criticism. Buñuel's bullfight is a philosophical discourse, and his films are the modern equivalent to Sade's philosophical novel. But Sade was an original philosopher and a middling artist: he did not realize that art, which loves rhythm and litany, excludes repetition and reiteration. Buñuel is an artist, and his films are subject not to poetic but philosophical reproach.

The reasoning which governs all Sade's work can be reduced to this idea: man is his instincts, and the true name of what we call God is fear and mutilated desire. Our morality is a codification of aggression and humiliation; reason itself is nothing but an instinct which knows itself to be instinct and which is afraid of being so. Sade did not set himself the task of proving that God does not exist: he took this for granted. He wanted to demonstrate what human relations would be like in an effectively atheist society. This is the essence of his originality and the unique character of his attempt. The archetype of a republic of truly free men is the Society of the Friends of Crime; of the true philosopher, the ascetic libertine who has managed to achieve impassiveness and who ignores laughter and tears alike. Sade's logic is total and circular: he destroys God but he does not respect man. His system can give rise to many criticisms, but not to that of incoherence. His negation is universal: if he affirms anything it is the right to destroy and be destroyed. Buñuel's criticism has a limit: man. All our crimes are the crimes of a phantom: God. Buñuel's theme is not man's guilt, but God's. This idea, present in all his films, is more explicit and direct in *L'Age d'or* and in *Viridiana*, which are for me, with *Los Olvidados*, his fullest and most perfect creations. If Buñuel's work is a criticism of the illusion of God, that distorting glass which will not let us see man as he is, what are men *really* like and what sense will the words love and fraternity have in a *really* atheist society?

Sade's answer does not satisfy Buñuel, of course. Nor do I believe that, at this time of day, he rests content with the descriptions which offer us philosophical or political utopias. Apart from the fact that these prophecies cannot be verified, at any event not yet, it is clear that they do not correspond to what we know about man, his history and his nature. To believe in an atheist society governed by natural harmony—a dream we have all had—would be today like repeating Pascal's wager, only in the opposite sense. More than a paradox, it would be an act of despair: it would command our admiration, not our assent. I do not know what answer Buñuel could give to these questions. Surrealism, which denied so many things, was motivated by a gale of generosity and faith. Among its ancestors are counted not only Sade and Lautréamont but also Fourier and Rousseau. And perhaps it is the last of these, at least for André Breton, who is the true origin of the movement: exaltation of passion, unlimited confidence in the natural powers of man. I do not know if Buñuel is closer to Sade or to Rousseau; it is more likely that both conduct an argument within him. Whatever his beliefs on this score, it is the case that in his films neither Sade's nor Rousseau's answer appears. Reticence, timidity, or disdain, his silence is troubling. It is troubling not only because it is the silence of one of the great artists of our time, but also because it is the silence of all the art of this first half-century. After Sade, as far as I know, no one has dared to discover an atheist society. Something is lacking in the work of our contemporaries: not God, but man without God.

Delhi, 1965

III CANNES, 1951:
LOS OLVIDADOS

I must have been about seventeen when I first heard of Luis Buñuel. I was a student at the National Preparatory School and I had just discovered, in the display cases of the Porrua and Robredo bookstores, near San Ildefonso, the books and magazines of the new literature. In one of these publications—*La gaceta literaria* (*The Literary Gazette*), which Ernesto Jiménez Caballero published in Madrid—I read an article on Buñuel and Dali. This article was illustrated by both of them, with reproductions of Dali's paintings and stills from their two films: *Un*

chien andalou and *L'Age d'or*. The stills excited me more deeply than the pictures by the Catalan painter: in the film images, the mixture of everyday reality and madness was more effective and explosive than in the mannerist illusionism of Dali. A few years later, in the summer of 1937 in Paris, I met Buñuel face to face.

One morning, at the door of the Spanish consulate, where I had gone with Pablo Neruda to pick up a visa, we bumped into him. Pablo stopped him and introduced us. It was a fleeting encounter. That same year I managed at last to see the two famous films, with the smell of cordite in the air: *Un chien andalou* and *L'Age d'or*. For me, the second film was, in the strict sense of the word, a revelation: the sudden appearance of a truth hidden and buried, but alive. I discovered that the age of gold is in each of us and that it has the face of passion.

Many years later, in 1951, again in Paris, I saw Luis Buñuel again at the house of some friends: Gaston and Betty Bouthoul. During that period I saw him quite often; he came to my house, and finally one day he called to entrust me with a mission: I was to present his film *Los Olvidados* at that year's Cannes Festival. I accepted enthusiastically, without hesitation. I had seen the film at a private showing with André Breton and other friends. A strange detail: the night of the showing, at the other end of the little projection room, Aragon, Sadoul, and others were present. When I saw them I thought for a moment that a pitched battle would ensue, as in the days of their youth. I exchanged glances with Elisa Breton, who showed signs of nervousness; but all and sundry sat down silently and a few minutes later the showing began. I think it was the first time Aragon and Breton had seen each other since their rift, twenty years before. The film moved me: it was animated by the same violent imagination and for the same implacable reason as *L'Age d'or*, but Buñuel, through using a very strict form, had managed a greater concentration. As we left, Breton praised the film, though he regretted that the director had conceded too much, at certain points, to the realist logic of the story at the expense of the poetry or, as he said, of the marvelous. For my part, I thought that *Los Olvidados* showed the way not to overcome superrealism—can anything be overcome in art and literature?—but to unravel it; I mean that Buñuel had found an exit from the superrealist aesthetic by inserting, in the traditional form of the narrative, the irrational images which spring up out of the dark side of man. (In those years I set myself a similar task in the more restricted domain of lyric poetry.) And here perhaps it is not out of place to say that in the best works of Buñuel a rare faculty is revealed, a faculty which could be called *synthetic imagination*, that is, totality and concentration.

As soon as I got to Cannes I met with the other Mexican delegate. He was a producer and exhibitor of Polish origin who lived in Paris. He said he was aware of my nomination as Mexican delegate to the festival and he pointed out that our country had sent another film to the festival. In fact, Buñuel was participating in the festival in his own right, invited by the French organizers. The Mexican delegate also told me that he had seen *Los Olvidados* in Paris, and it seemed to him, despite its artistic merits, an esoteric film, aestheticist and at times incomprehensible. In his judgment, it had no chance whatsoever of winning any prize. He added that various Mexican high functionaries, as well as numerous intellectuals and journalists, were against the showing at Cannes of a film that denigrated Mexico. This last point was unfortunately true, and Buñuel has referred to the subject in his memoirs (*My Last Sigh*), though discreetly, without naming his critics. I will follow his example, but not without stressing that, in this attitude of theirs, the two evils which at that time our progressive intellectuals suffered from came together: nationalism and socialist realism.

The skepticism of my colleague in the Mexican delegation was made up for by the enthusiasm and goodwill that various friends, all admirers of Buñuel, showed, among them the legendary Langlois, director of the Cinématheque de Paris, and two young superrealists, Kyrou and Benayoun, who put out an avant-garde magazine, *L'Age du cinéma*. We visited many notable artists who lived in the Côte d'Azur, inviting them to the event at which the film was to be shown. Almost all of them accepted. One of those most keen to show himself in favor of Buñuel and of free art was, to my surprise, the painter Chagall. On the other hand, Picasso proved evasive and reticent; in the end, he didn't show up. I recalled his hardly friendly attitude to Apollinaire in the matter of the Phoenician statuettes. Most generous of all was the poet Jacques Prévert. He lived in Vence, a few kilometers from Cannes. Langlois and I went to see him, we told him our worries, and a few days later he sent us a poem in praise of Buñuel which we hurried into print. I believe it caused a certain stir among the critics and journalists attending the festival.

I wrote a little essay as a kind of introduction. Since we had no money we mimeographed it. On the day of the showing I handed it out to all comers at the door of the theater. A few days later a Paris newspaper printed it. Buñuel's film immediately occasioned many articles, commentaries, and discussions. *Le Monde* praised it to the skies, but *L'Humanité* called it "a negative film." Those were the years of socialist realism, and the *positive message* was exalted as the central value of works of art. I remember the furious argument I had one night shortly after the showing with Georges Sadoul. He told me Buñuel had *deserted* the true realism and that he was paddling, though talentedly, in the sewage of bourgeois pessimism. I replied that his use of the word *desert* revealed that his idea of art was worthy of a sergeant and that with the theory of socialist realism the intention was to conceal the null Soviet social reality. . . . The rest is known: *Los Olvidados* did not get the grand prix, but with that film begins Buñuel's second and great creative period.

Mexico, 1983

JORGE GUILLÉN

Jorge Guillén is a Spaniard from Castile, which doesn't mean he's more Spanish than the Spaniards of other regions but that he is Spanish in a different way. He is no purist: Guillén is a European Spaniard and belongs to an historical moment in which Spanish culture was opening out to the thought and art of Europe. But unlike Ortega, who enlivened and inspired that group, Guillén was closer to France than to Germany. He pursued his university studies in Paris, where he was married first and where he taught. He also gave courses at Oxford. He returned to Spain and promptly became a leading figure of a generation which Gerardo Diego introduced in 1925 in a celebrated anthology. It was a generation parallel to the one that in Mexico gathered around the magazine *Contemporáneos*. The Civil War scattered the Spanish poets. Guillén lived for years in the United States.

For much of his life he has been a university professor. He has lived for long stretches in Italy, where he married for the second time. A whole European. Also a complete Spanish-American: he knows our continent and has friends in all our countries.

His work is extensive and almost entirely in verse. Three books: *Cántico (Canticle)*, *Clamor (Tumult)*, and *Homenaje (Homage)*. The subtitles are illuminating: *Cántico: Fe de vida (Faith in Life)*— affirmation of being and affirmation of what is. This book has had very great influence on our language. *Clamor: Tiempo de historia (The Time of History)*—the poet in the corridors—errors and horrors—of contemporary history. *Homenaje: Reunión de vidas (Joining of Lives)*—the poet not among men or confronting them but with them. And above all with women: Guillén is a poet for whom woman exists. I am sure he would agree if he heard me say that woman is the highest form of being. *Reunión de vidas*, with poets living as well as dead: in that book Guillén converses with his masters, his antecedents in the poetic art, and his contemporaries and successors. When he began writing he was thought a severe poet; now we realize that he has also been an extremely fecund poet: in 1973 he published a new book, simply called *Y otros poemas (And Other Poems)*.

Guillén belongs to a group of writers who knew they were part of a tradition that transcends linguistic frontiers. All of them felt that they were not only German, French, Italian, or Spanish but European. The European consciousness, a victim of nationalisms, is progressively attenuated until it almost vanishes in the nineteenth century. Its rebirth, at the beginnings of this century, is something Europe had not experienced since the eighteenth century. Examples of this sensibility include Rilke, Valéry Larbaud, Ungaretti, Eliot. Here I should mention two Latin Americans: Alfonso Reyes and Jorge Luis Borges. It is instructive to note that all of them wrote in their native language and in French—except Borges, who has written in English. In those years Paris was still the center, if not of the world, at least of art and literature. . . . In that Paris of the first third of the century Guillén spent decisive formative years. The Paris of Huidobro had been one of revolt in art and poetry: Picasso, Reverdy, Tzara, Arp, the beginnings of surrealism. Guillén is nearer to the *Nouvelle Revue Française* and, above all, to *Commerce*, the great poetry magazine edited by Paul Valéry, Leon Paul Fargue, and Valéry Larbaud—the great Larbaud, friend of Gómez de la Serna, Reyes, Güiraldes.

Because of his classical bent Guillén suggests a Mediterranean Eliot. But literary essays and critical writing do not occupy the same place in Guillén's work as they do in Eliot's. And there is something else which radically distinguishes him from Eliot: in his work there is scarcely a trace of Christianity. His subject is sensual and intellectual: the world touched by the senses and the mind. Profoundly Mediterranean poetry, Guillén is very near to Valéry. He was his friend, experienced his influence, and his translation of "Le cimetière marine" is a masterpiece. All the same, the similarities between Valéry and Guillén do not cancel out the deep differences. Valéry is a spirit of prodigious insight, one of the truly luminous minds of this century. He is a great writer endowed with two qualities which in others appear opposed: intellectual rigor and sensuality. But these admirable and unique gifts are as if lost in a kind of vacancy: unsupported, they lack world. The I, the consciousness, has swallowed the world. This evaporation of reality, is it the price the skeptic must pay if he wants to make sense to himself? I doubt it. Hume was no less a skeptic, and yet his work has an architecture which Valéry's lacks. Valéry's powers of deconstruction were greater than his powers of construction. His *Cahiers* are an imposing ruin. Valéry was a most powerful spiritual lever which lacked a pivot point. Guillén's critical and analytical powers are not as great as Valéry's, but his spiritual lever did not lack a pivot.

For Guillén reality is what we touch and see: faith in the senses is the poet's true faith. This provides him common ground with certain painters. Not the realists but rather an artist like Juan Gris, in whom the rigor of abstraction is fused with a fidelity to the physical object. In Guillén, good Mediterranean that he is, sensuality is dominant, and this draws him toward another great painter, Matisse. These names, it seems to me, trace Guillén's spiritual profile: his lucidity calls Valéry to mind; his almost ascetic rigor before the object allies him with Juan Gris; the line which swerves like a feminine river evokes Matisse. But the light which illuminates his poetry is that of the Castilian plains, the light which shines down to us from Fray Luis Ponce de León and his Horatian odes.

Guillén returned to Spain in 1924. He was thirty years old. He had not yet published a book. He was a late developer, unlike Lorca and Alberti. The panorama of Spanish poetry in those days was extremely rich. Never since the seventeenth century had Spain had so many excellent poets. That was the best period of Juan Ramón Jiménez. It was also the period of his influence on the young writers. Juan Ramón was writing a simple, inspired poetry in the traditional vein of the Spanish lyric: songs, romances, *coplas*, and other popular forms. Short poems, almost exclamations; fresh poems, sudden fountains. Poetry of popular rhythms and yet aristocratic, refined, and as is clear to us today, a boneless poetry, without architecture, excessively subjective. Though the young poets followed Juan Ramón, their images came from creationism and ultraism. Huidobro's system of metaphor had stirred the poets of Latin America and Spain a few years earlier. A strong but very Spanish amalgam of traditionalism and avant-garde: Alberti composed madrigals to the train ticket and Salinas songs to the radiator.

There was much talk in those years of "pure poetry." Juan Ramón defined it as the simple, the plain and refined: a word reduced to the essential. In fact, Juan Ramón was not defining "pure poetry" so much as his own poetry. Guillén was returning from France, where the notion of "pure poetry" was also in the ascendant. The French conception was more rigorous. Abbé Bremond had defined "pure poetry" with a nondefinition: it was the undefinable, what is beyond sound and sense, something which was confused with prayer and ecstasy. Though for Valéry poetry was neither gibberish nor prayer, his definitions too were, in their apparent simplicity, enigmatic: poetry was all that which could not be said in prose. But what can't be said in prose? In a letter to a friend Guillén defines his position in brief. It is typical of Guillén to formulate his poetic in a letter to a friend: Huidobro had launched various manifestos, and others of us have written essays and even books. It is worth quoting part of his letter, well known though it is:

> Bremond has been and remains useful. He represents the popular apologetic, like a poet-catechist for Sunday morning. And his lecture is a sermon. But how far all this mysticism is, with its metaphysical and ineffable phantom, from pure poetry, according to Poe, to Valéry and the young poets of there and here! Bremond speaks of poetry in the poet, of a *poetic state*, and that's already a bad sign. No, no. There is no poetry but that achieved in the poem and there is no way to set against the poem an *ineffable state* which is corrupted when it is carried out. . . . Pure poetry is mathematics and chemistry—nothing more—in the good sense of that expression suggested by Valéry and which some young mathematicians and chemists have made their own, understanding it in a different sense, but always within that initial, fundamental direction. Valéry himself repeated it to me, once, one morning in the rue de Villejust. Pure poetry is all that remains in the poem after all that is not poetry has been eliminated. *Pure* is the same as *simple* in chemical terms. . . . Since I call *pure, simple*, I come down resolutely on the side of composed, complex poetry, the poem with poetry and other human things. In sum, quite a pure poetry, *ma non*

troppo, if one takes as the unit of comparison the *simple* element in its greatest inhuman and superhuman theoretical rigor.

Guillén denied that there were "poetic states": poetry is in the poem, is a verbal deed. This attitude radically separated him not only from Bremond but, at the other extreme, from the surrealists, who attributed more importance to the poetic experience than to the act of writing poems. Guillén was aware that, whatever else, a purely poetic poetry would be quite boring. And something more serious: it was linguistically impossible since language is by nature impure. A "pure poetry" would be one in which language had ceased to be language. The idea of "pure poetry" was very much of its period. Years before, physics had tried to isolate the ultimate components of matter. For their part, the cubist painters reduced objects to a series of relations on a plane. Following the example of the physicists and painters, as Jakobson has more than once recalled, the linguists had attempted to discover the ultimate elements of language, the signifying particles. This intellectual orientation was powerfully manifest in the work of Edmund Husserl, the phenomenologist. The philosophers of this persuasion, too, attempted to reduce things to their essences, and thus regional ontologies of the chair, the pencil, the claw, the hand were made. Unfortunately, these ontologies almost always ended in expressions such as these: The chair is the chair, poetry is poetry (or: all that is not prose). Phenomenology issues, I'm afraid, in tautologies. But tautology is, perhaps, the only metaphysical affirmation which men can reach. The most we can say about being is that it is.

MOST CRITICS HAVE INSISTED on the ontological character of "Mas alla," the opening poem of *Cantico*: affirming what is and affirming being. I have always looked a little distrustfully

171

at philosophical explanations of poetry. Still, in this instance, interpretation can serve us as a point of departure for a fuller understanding of the poem, so long as we do not forget even for a moment that "Mas alla" is not a philosophical treatise but a poem. The ideas of the poem interest and arouse us not because they are true but because Guillén has made them poetically true. The axis on which "Mas alla" turns, and more generally, the axis of all the poetry in *Cántico*, is an affirmation which appears at the beginning and end of the poem: *quiero ser* (I want to be). Two-edged phrase: I want being and I want to be. This double and universal wanting is already present in Plato: all beings want to be because the supreme good is being. That is why Saint Augustine thought that evil was nothing but the absence of being.

Generally speaking, also since Plato, being is identified with essence. What is the being of the chair, table, star? Its essence, its idea. Ultimate realities, essential realities, are ideas: intellectual forms we can contemplate, whether in the starry sky or in the space, at once ideal and subject to the senses, of the geometric bodies. But Guillén's poem does not affirm being as essence or as idea but as passing: being is blood and time, eternity suspended. An eternity which is manifest in dates, places, and circumstances: today, Monday, in this room, in the morning. Is this a form of materialism? No, the ultimate reality is neither material nor ideal: it is a wanting, a relationship, an interchange. We have before us a paradoxical realism since it supports itself by affirming the instant as eternity.

Guillén's realism looks like relativism. It is established on flux, that is, on time. When the poem begins, huge time surrounds the sleeper. Later, made energy, it manifests itself in things. That energy moves things and changes them. The world is relation because it is time which is movement which is passing which is change. Movement of one thing toward another and change of one thing into another. Here Guillén's universalizing strategy comes into play: being—an absolute—becomes relative, becomes particular and is manifest in this and that; this and that are relative, are time, are instants, but each instant is all time, each instant is a totality. The now becomes forever, a forever that is happening now and is happening for ever. Here is wherever, and wherever is the center of the universe. First movement: being is not an essence or an idea: it is a passing, an energy crystallized in a here and now. Second movement: here is central, the point toward which all points converge; and the now is an always which is an instant, a suspended eternity. Man is the agent of this trans-mutation. Or rather: man's desire to be is. The desire is his and his alone: at the same time, it is the desire of all creatures and all things. It is a universal wanting. What is more, the plural universe is a desire to be in unison.

Man is the point of intersection of this plural universe of desire, and that is why each man is central. But man is central not because he is the creation of the demiurge. Man is not king of creation nor the favorite son of the creator. Man is the point of intersection between chance and necessity. I use deliberately the title of the book by the biologist Jacques Monod—*Chance and Necessity*—because there is a curious coincidence between Guillén's poetic thought and contemporary biology. For Guillén, man's being is at the same time the expression of universal totality—his body follows its circuit well, as those of the stars do—and the result of a chance collision of forces and energies: atoms, cells, acids. Another biologist, Francois Jacob, says that cells have no function but to reproduce, copy, and duplicate themselves. We might say that they are in love with themselves, like Narcissus and like Luzbel. Sometimes, when they copy themselves, by a well-under-stood principle of physics, changes occur. These are mutants. These mutants pass through the strainer of natural selection; some vanish, and others, as they grow strong, perpetuate them-selves until they give rise to new species. But the cells of Jacob and Monod are a desire to be which only wants to be, while Guillén's will to be is, like that of all men, a desire to be which contemplates itself, reflects itself, and, above all, speaks. It is an accord which does not recognize itself as such. Man rescues the instant when he speaks it, names it. The present endures not only and exclusively because, like the cells, it repeats itself, but because it sees itself through the moment. In that momentary apparition, consciousness accedes to a kind of vertiginous eternity—and names it. An eternity which lasts as long as it takes the poet to say it and us to hear it. It is enough.

Man—that universal desire of being and that desire of universal being—is a moment of change, one of the forms in which energy is manifest. That moment and that form are transitory, circumstantial: here and now. That moment will disappear, that form will be scattered. Nonetheless, that moment includes all moments, is all moments; that form binds itself with all forms and is in every part. How do we know this? We know it without knowing it. We feel it when we live certain experiences. For example, when we wake up. Except that really to wake up we must take account of the fact that the world in which we wake up is a world which wakes up with us. Without eyes and soul man could not know that each minute is on the crest of time and at the center of space. But eyes and soul are not enough: the world is incomprehensible, the ultimate reality is invisible, untouchable. No matter: we have language. By means of the words we get close to things, we call them *evidences*, *prodigies*, *riddles*, *transcendencies*. Language is a dike against nameless chaos. The world of relations which is the universe is a verbal world: we wander among things which are names. We ourselves are names. Landscapes of names which time unceasingly destroys. Wasted names which we have to invent anew each century, each generation, every morning when we wake up. Poetry is the process by which man names the world and names himself. That is why man is the legend of reality. And I would add, the legend of himself.

Guillén's here and now resemble the instant which dissolves

all instants. It is the instant of lovers and also that of mystics, especially Eastern ones, with which Guillén is perhaps not acquainted, and whom he would probably disapprove of if he knew them. That instant annuls the contradiction between this and that, past and future, negation and affirmation. It is not the union, the marriage of contraries, but their scattering. On this vision of the other aspect of being—the blank aspect: vacancy—it is not easy to erect a metaphysic. But it is possible to build a wisdom and above all a poetics. It is an experience which we have all lived and which some have thought. Poets are those who, whatever their beliefs, language, and age, manage to express it.

In *Mediciones*, 1979

TWO NOTES ON JOSÉ REVUELTAS: CHRISTIANITY AND REVOLUTION

FIRST NOTE

When the armed struggle ceased and what has come to be called "the constructive phase of the Mexican Revolution" began, two different forms of artistic expression, the novel and painting, avidly addressed themselves to the recent past. The consequences of this engagement have been the "Mexican school of painting" and the "Novel of the Revolution." Over the last twenty years the novel has served to express the authors' nostalgias, hopes, and disillusions with the revolution, rather than any more literary undertakings. Technically poor, these works are more picturesque than descriptive, more in the nature of genre writing than realism.... The novelists of the revolution, and among them the great myopic talent of Mariano Azuela, blinded by the frenzy of gunpowder or by that other frenzy of the corrupt generals' diamonds, have reduced their theme to that: many deaths, many crimes and lies. And a superficial stage set of burned villages, maddening jungles, and godless deserts. In this way they have mutilated fictional reality—the only reality that matters to the true novelist—by reducing it to a pure chronicle or a framed portrayal of customs. All the "Novels of the Revolution" have been narratives and chronicles, even those of Mariano Azuela. (Valéry Larbaud declared that Martín Luis Guzmán reminded him of Tacitus: a strange way to praise a novelist!)

The next generation has hardly attempted the novel. Made up as it is by a group of literati, poets, and essayists, it has shown a degree of repugnance, if not disdain, for the realities which surround it. The novel has been the Cinderella of these writers, who rally under the banner of curiosity and evasion. After them, there have been isolated attempts: those of the most recent group of Mexican writers (Juan de la Cabada, Efrén Hernández, Rubén Salazar Mallén, Andrés Henestrosa, Rafael Solana, Francisco Tario). Almost all of them evince a marked preference for that hard and strict genre, the short story. Just as in painting the generation of "muralists" has been succeeded by a group of young artists which a patronizing North American critic dubbed the "little masters," so these new Mexican prose writers, successors to the "Novelists of the Revolution," have excelled above all in the writing of short stories and narratives. One of Juan de la Cabada's books, *Paséo de mentiras* (*Passage of Lies*), brings together in a few pages some stories and a novella which make him, up to now, the most interesting and enigmatic of all; one novel, *Camino de perfección* (*Road of Perfection*), and particularly some bitter and harsh stories, lead one to believe that Rubén Salazar Mallén also has the necessary talent to give Mexico a real novel.

The most ambitious and impassioned—and the youngest, too— is José Revueltas (twenty-seven years old, affiliated from the age of fourteen with the Communist Party; his political ideas have given him a chance to get to know the insides of the country's jails several times, in the time of President Rodríguez). José Revueltas has published a first novel, *El luto humano* (*Human Sorrow*), which has received an award in a national competition. Before that he had written some mysterious, stammering stories; a short novel, *El quebranto*,* and a narrative, *Los muros de agua* (*The Walls of Water*), in which he tells of the life of a penal colony in the Pacific. (He was imprisoned there for two years, before he reached the age of twenty.) Revueltas's novel has aroused both the most ardent praise and the sourest criticism. A Marxist critic has charged him with pessimism, but other enthusiasts have been quick to cite Dostoevski.

El luto humano tells a dramatic story: a group of peasants goes on strike at an "irrigation system" established by the Mexican Revolutionary government. The strike and the consequent drought cause the government plan to fail and the exodus begins. Only three families insist on staying on in that deserted place. One day the river, dry until that time, swells and breaks its banks and a flood isolates the characters of the novel on a rooftop. Alcohol, hunger, and jealousy finish them off. The novel opens when the river begins to swell and ends just as the buzzards settle down to devour the dying. All these events take place in a period of a few days. But the novel scarcely alludes to what the peasants actually do to escape the flood; Revueltas prefers to tell us what they think, what they remember, what they feel. Often he displaces his characters; in their place he expounds his own doubts, his faith and his despair, his opinions about death or about Mexican religiosity. The action is interrupted each time a character, before dying, summarizes his life. . . . A constant religious concern invades the work: Mexicans, pious by nature, and lovers of blood, have been deprived of their religion, without the Catholic faith having been enough to satisfy their hard thirst for eternity.

---

*It was never published in full, except for the first chapter (*Taller* 2, April 1939), because Revueltas lost the manuscript.

Adam, a murderer, who believes himself to be the embodiment of Fate, and Natividad, a murdered leader, symbolize, in very religious terms, the past and future of Mexico. Between them move the rancorous present-day Mexicans, and their taciturn women represent the earth, thirsty for water and blood, a baptism that combines, together with agricultural fertility rites, ancient Aztec and Christian rites. In the closing pages the author tries to convince himself—more than the reader—that by a better use of natural resources and a better distribution of wealth, this religiosity without hope, this blind love of death, will vanish from the Mexican soul. The novel is clearly contaminated with sociology, religion, and ancient and modern Mexican history. There is some contamination in the language, which is at times brilliant, at times strangely turgid.

These faults damn the work, but not its author. Because, oddly, the reader feels himself infected with the same fascination to which the novelist is prey. Revueltas feels a kind of religious revulsion, of love composed of horror and repulsion, for Mexico. True, Revueltas has not written a novel, but, all the same, he has cast light into himself. Seduced as much by the myths of Mexico as by its realities, he has made himself a part of that drama which he attempts to depict. Endowed with talent, imaginative force, quite uncommon vigor and sensibility—and devoured by a haste which does not let him, it would seem, linger over his faults—José Revueltas is now ready to write a novel. In this attempt he frees himself of all his phantoms, all his doubts and opinions. As is the case with much Mexican painting, which reveals a great vigor that often remains outside the picture, beyond the frame, Revueltas has brought together all his great modeling and prophetic power, but without managing to apply it to his object: the novel. In short, for what am I reproaching Revueltas? I reproach him—I now realize—for his youth, since all those defects, that lack of soberness in the language, that desire to say it all at once, that lack of concentration and that reluctance to trim the useless wings of words, ideas, and situations, that absence of discipline—within and without—these are nothing but the faults of youth. In any event, Revueltas is the first writer among us who has tried to create a deep work, remote from genre writing, superficiality, and the cut-price psychology which dominate today. Perhaps nothing will remain of this work of his but its spirit: isn't this enough for a young man who is just starting, and starting us, on the task of creating for ourselves an imaginative world, strange and disturbingly personal?

Sur, July 1943

SECOND NOTE

When I reread the preceding note, which Luis Mario Schneider dug out of an old issue of *Sur*, I immediately felt the need to clarify, correct, and extend it. It is one beginner's criticism of another beginner; what is more, it is far too cutting and categorical. My excuse is that those faults are frequent among the young. I end by reproaching Revueltas for his youth, and that censure is perfectly applicable to the opinion I held at that time. Youth does not justify other errors. For instance, in the first paragraph I condemn the novelists of the Mexican Revolution. That was a silliness: among them there are two excellent writers, Martín Luis Guzmán and Mariano Azuela. Both were masters of their art. Martín Luis Guzmán's prose, bright as that of a Roman historian, has a kind of classical transparence: its subject is terrible, but he traces it with a calm, firm rhythm. Azuela was not "a great myopic talent"; nor was he dull: he was a lucid writer, in control of his resources, and he explored many roads which others have traveled since. But when I wrote my note on *El luto humano* (1943), the novel of the revolution had turned itself from a movement into a school: the invention was now a recipe. In this sense I was not wrong: the appearance of *El luto humano*, published a few years before *Al filo del agua* by Augustín Yañez (1947), was a break and a beginning. Despite its imperfections, Revueltas's novel set something in motion which is not yet exhausted.

My analysis of *El luto humano* is too brisk. I point out with excessive severity the narrator's unskillful devices and the frequency with which his voice displaces that of his characters. Those defects are due, at least in part, to the difficulty and novelty of what Revueltas was setting out to say and what he managed to say more felicitously years later. The young novelist wanted to use the new techniques of the North American novel (the Faulkner of *The Wild Palms* is constantly present) to write a chronicle that was at once epic and symbolic, about an episode which seemed to him to possess the quality of a revolutionary exemplum. The purpose was contradictory: Faulkner's realism (perhaps all realism) implies a pessimistic view of man and of his earthly destiny; in its turn, Revueltas's epic chronicle is undermined by religious symbolism, for lack of a better expression. The peasants fight for land and water, but the novelist continually suggests that that fight alludes to another, one not entirely of this world. Though my note stresses the religiosity of Revueltas, it does not describe its paradoxical character: a vision of Christianity *within* his Marxist atheism. Revueltas lived his Marxism as a Christian, and that is why he lived it, in Unamuno's sense, as agony, doubt, and negation.

In speaking of the religiosity of the Mexican people, I mention "rancor," an inexact word. I attribute it to the great catastrophe of the Conquest, which deprived the Indians not only of their world but of their otherworld: that of their gods and mythologies. Still, when with the key of baptism it unlocked the gates of heaven and hell for them, Catholicism paradoxically gave them the possibility of coming to terms with their old religion. Perhaps Revueltas thought that, "on a higher historical plain," revolutionary Marxism would perform in the face of Christianity the same

181

function that Christianity performed in the face of the pre-Columbian religions. This idea would explain the importance of the Christian symbolism in the novel. Moreover, he was always fascinated by popular beliefs and myths. A friend told me how once, half in jest, half seriously, it occurred to Revueltas to celebrate a marriage rite not before the altar of the Virgin of Guadalupe but before the goddess Coatlicue in the Museum of Anthropology. I remember too that on the night of the 1971 Corpus Christi massacre, when a number of friends were gathered at Carlos Fuentes's house and we discussed what we might do, Revueltas approached me and with an undefinable smile on his face whispered in my ear: "Let's all go dance before the Holy Lord of Chalma!" A phrase reveals a man: "Atheism," André Breton once told me, "is an act of faith." The *witticisms* of Revueltas were oblique confessions.

At the end of my note I point to the real significance of *El luto humano*: "Revueltas has not written a novel, but . . . he has cast light into himself." Today I would say: that work was a stage in his pilgrimage, a real Way of the Cross, toward the light. And this is the source of the central question, which Revueltas faced bravely from his very short novel, *El quebranto*, and which he never stopped asking himself: What light, the light *here*, or *there*? Perhaps here is there, perhaps revolutions are nothing but the road that here travels toward there. Revueltas's action seems to be secretly inspired by this idea. He was a militant revolutionary, novelist, and author of philosophical and political essays. As a militant he was a dissident who criticized with identical passion capitalism and bureaucratic "socialism"; the same duality is evident in his novels, stories, and essays. Thus, on the one hand, there is a remarkable continuity between his life and his work: it is impossible to separate the novelist from the militant and the militant from the author of texts of philosophical, aesthetic, and political criticism; on the other hand, that unity contains a fracture, an excision. Revueltas was in a continual dialogue—or more precisely, a permanent dispute—with his philosophical, aesthetic, and political ideas. His criticism of Communist orthodoxy was self-criticism at the same time. His case is not unique, of course; on the contrary, it is more and more common: the dissidence of Marxist intellectuals is one expression, perhaps the central one, of the universal crisis of that doctrine. But there is something that sets Revueltas's doubts and criticisms apart from the others: the tone, the religious passion. And there is something more: the questions which Revueltas time and again asked himself make no sense and cannot be answered except within a religious frame of reference. Not that of just any religion but specifically that of Christianity.

For Westerners the opposition between atheism and religion cannot be resolved. This has not been the case with other civilizations: in its strictest and purest form, Buddhism is atheist. And yet that atheism does not root out the divine: like all beings, without excepting men or the Buddha himself, the gods are bubbles, reflections of emptiness. Buddhism is a radical critique of reality and the human condition: the true reality, *sunyata*, is an undefinable state in which being and nonbeing, the real and the unreal, cease to be at odds and, in coming together, annul themselves. Thus history is nothing but shadow play, illusion—like everything else. This is also why Buddhist religious observance is essentially contemplative. By contrast, for Christianity the incarnation of Jesus and his sacrifice are deeds that are at once supernatural and historical. Not only does divine revelation unfold in history, but history is the testing ground for Christians: souls triumph and are lost here, in this world. The Marxist Revueltas takes on the Christian heritage with all its consequences: the weight of human history. The nexus between Christianity and Marxism is history; both are doctrines which identify with the historical process. The condition in which Marxism is possible is the same as that for Christianity: action on this world. And the rivalry between Marxism and Christianity is manifest here on earth: to fulfill himself and his mission, revolutionary man has to evict God from history. The first revolutionary act is the critique of Heaven. The relation between Marxism and Christianity implies, at the same time, a bond and a breach. Buddhism— in general terms, all Eastern thought—ignores or disdains history. At the same time, immersed in an atmosphere of the divine, surrounded by gods, it does not acknowledge the notion of a unique creator God. Oriental atheism is not really atheistic; in a strict sense, only Jews, Christians, and Moslems can be atheists: they are believers in a single creator God. Bloch very rightly said: "Only a true Christian can be a good atheist; only a true atheist can be a good Christian."

The Christian Marxism of Revueltas can only be understood from the double perspective I have just sketched. In the first place, the idea of history conceived as a process endowed with meaning and direction; secondly, irreducible atheism. Now, between history and atheism a further opposition opens out: if God disappears, history ceases to mean. Christian atheism is tragic because, as Nietzsche saw it, it is a negation of meaning. For Dostoevski, if there is no God, everything is permissible, everything is possible; but if everything is possible, nothing is: the infinity of possibilities annuls them and resolves them in impossibility. In the same way: the absence of God makes everything thinkable; but everything equals nothing: everything and nothing are not thinkable. Atheism sets us face to face with the unthinkable and the impossible; that is why it is terrifying and, literally, unbearable. Also, that is why we have installed other deities in God's vacant niche: Reason, Progress. These principles come down to earth, become incarnate and turn into the secret activators of history. They are our Christs: the nation, the proletariat, the race. In Revueltas's novel, the old man is called Adam, like our father; and the new man, the collective Christ, is called Nativity. The history of the Son of Man begins with the Nativity and culminates with the Sacrifice; the Revolution obeys the same logic. That logic is rational, "scientific": historical materialism; and it is supernatural: transcendence. The "scientific" is explicit; the supernatural, implicit. Divine transcendence disappears, but, surreptitiously, by means of revolutionary action it continues to function. As Bloch also said, revolution is "to transcend without transcendence."

The hostility between Marxism and Christianity never entirely disappears but it is attenuated if the terms change places. For Christianity we men are sons of Adam, the child of God. In the beginning is God, who is not only the giver of meaning but the creator of life. God is before history and after it: he is the beginning and the end. For a Christian Marxist like Bloch or Revueltas, God cannot be before; in fact, God does not exist: the original, primordial reality is man or, better said, human society. But historical man is hardly man at all; to realize himself, truly to be man, he must pass through the trials of history, must triumph over it and transform its fatal course into liberty. Revolution makes men of men—and more than men: man's future is to be God. Christianity was the humanizing of God; revolution promises divinity to man. Abrupt change of places: God is not before but after, not the creator of men but their creature. Bloch alters the Biblical phrase and says *I am what I will be* (Ernst Bloch, *L'athéisme dans le christianisme*, Gallimard, 1978).

Revueltas never formulated his ideas with Bloch's clarity, but the *temper* of his writings and his life corresponds to this agonizing and contradictory vision of Marxism and Christianity. Of course, he reached these attitudes independently and by his own route. It was not philosophy that guided him but his personal experience. In the first place, the religion of his childhood; then his interest in Mexican common life, all of it impregnated with religiosity; and finally, his philosophical and poetic temperament. This last was decisive: Revueltas asked himself philosophical questions which Marxism—as among others Kolakowski and Bloch himself have recognized—cannot answer except with scientistic commonplaces. In fact, those questions have only metaphysical and religious answers. Metaphysics, after Hume and Kant, is forbidden to us moderns. Thus Revueltas resorts intuitively and with passion, in a movement back to the earliest elements in his being, to the religious answers, mingled with the millenarian ideas and hopes of the revolutionary movement. Though philosophy enthralled him, he was above all a creative artist. His religious temperament drew him to communism, which he saw as the way of sacrifice and communion; that same temperament, inseparable from the love of truth and the good, led him at the end of his life to a criticism of bureaucratic "socialism" and Marxist clericalism.

Marxism has turned into an ideology and today functions as a pseudoreligion. The transformation of a philosophy into an ideology and of this into a religion is not a new phenomenon: the same thing happened with Neoplatonism and Gnosticism. Nor is the transformation of a religion into a political power and of a priesthood into a clerical bureaucracy anything new: Roman Catholicism has known these perversions. The historical peculiarity of communism is in the fact that it is not really a religion but an ideology that works as though it were a science, the Science; thus, it is not a church but a party which does not resemble other parties so much as the militant orders and brotherhoods of the Catholics and Moslems. Communist parties begin as little sects but as soon as they grow, they turn into closed churches. (I use the plural because in the Communist movement schisms and divisions proliferate.) Each church believes that it possesses universal truth; this pretension would not be perilous were it not for the fact that the bureaucracies which govern these groups are motivated by an equally universal desire to dominate and proselytize. Each member of each church is a missionary and each missionary a potential inquisitor. Revueltas's religiousness was far removed from these ideological fanaticisms; his true spiritual affinities are to be found on the other side, near the primitive Christians, the fourth-century Gnostics, and the Protestant rebels and revolutionaries of the Reformation. Within the Catholic Church he would have been as much a heretic as he was within the Communist orthodoxy. His Marxism was not a system but a passion, not a faith but a doubting and, to use Bloch's terminology, a hope.

It was no less difficult for Revueltas to live with himself than it was for him to live with his Communist comrades. For years he tried to be a disciplined militant, and each attempt ended in a breach and expulsion. He used the Hegelian dialectic to postpone the definitive breach; like so many others, he told himself that evil is a snare of history so that it might the better fulfill itself, that denial is a moment in the process which inevitably turns into affirmation, that the revolutionary tyrants are tyrants in order to protect liberty, and that—as the Spanish theologians of the seventeenth century and in the twentieth century Prosecutor Vishinsky and the Bolsheviks tried in 1936 and 1938 have brilliantly proven—the guilty are innocent and the innocent guilty. These are the riddles of divine will or of historical necessity. The justification of evil began with Plato; in his retractions and recantations, Revueltas did nothing more than pursue a two-thousand-year-old tradition. As the Neoplatonist Proclus said, matter itself "is good, despite being infinite, obscure and formless." (For the ancients infinity was an imperfection since it lacked form.) But the resources of dialectics are exhausted while the evil expands without ceasing. In the end Revueltas had to confront the reality of bolshevism and his own reality. He did not resolve this conflict—who has ever managed to do that?—but he had the courage to formulate it and think it through. He loyally lived out his inner contradiction: his atheist Christianity, his agonized Marxism. Many praise the courage with which he suffered prisons and hardships on account of his ideas. It's true, but it must be borne in mind, too, that Revueltas practiced another kind of heroism, no less difficult and austere: intellectual heroism.

His work is uneven. Some pages seem to be rough drafts rather than definitive texts; others are remarkable and entitle him to a unique and separate place in Mexican literature: *Los dias terrenales*, *Los errores*, *El apando*, and, above all, the stories of *Dios en la tierra* and *Dormir en tierra*, many of them admirable. But the literary excellence of these works, considerable though it is, does not altogether explain his attractiveness. In our world everything is relative, good and evil, pleasure and pain. Though the majority are content, a few rebel and, possessed by a god or by a devil, demand *everything*. They thirst and hunger for the absolute. Don't ask me to define it: the absolute is by definition undefinable. Revueltas suffered from that hunger and that thirst; to satisfy them he was writer and he was revolutionary. If I look among modern Mexicans for a kindred spirit, I have to go to the opposite ideological camp and to an earlier generation: to José Vasconcelos. Like Revueltas, he had a passionate nature but was unable to subject his passion to discipline; he was a writer of impulses and prophecies, copious and careless, sometimes dull and other times luminous. For both, political action and metaphysical adventure, historical polemic and meditation, were interconnected. They united the active life with the contemplative or, more accurately, the speculative life: in their works there is not really disinterested contemplation—what I take to be the highest wisdom—but meditation, reflection, and, in his best moments, spiritual flight. The work of Vasconcelos is larger and richer than that of Revueltas, but no deeper or more intense. But the point is, they belong to the same psychic family. They are the opposite of Reyes, who made an absolute of harmony; and of Gorostiza, who adored perfection with so exclusive a love that he preferred to be silent rather than write something less than perfect.

Despite their spiritual resemblance, Vasconcelos and Revueltas took very different roads. Nourished on Plotinus and believing in his mission as a crowned philosopher, Vasconcelos felt he had been sent down from on high: that is why he was an educator;

Revueltas believed in the rebel apostles and saw himself as an emissary of the lower world: that is why he was a revolutionary. The spiritualist Vasconcelos never doubted: the devil—that spirit of denial and patron of philosophers—did not tempt him: the world tempted him (power) and the flesh (women). Vasconcelos confessed that he had desired his neighbor's wife and that he had fornicated with her, but he never admitted that he had made a mistake. The only sins which the materialist Revueltas confessed to were sins of the spirit: doubts, denials, errors, pious lies. In the end he repented and undertook the criticism of his ideas and of the dogmas in which he had believed. Vasconcelos did not repent; he exalted Christian humility the better to cover his foes with invectives; Revueltas, in the name of Marxist philosophy, undertook an examination of his conscience which Saint Augustine and Pascal would have appreciated and which impresses me on two counts: for the scrupulous honesty with which he performed it and for the subtlety and depth of his analysis. Vasconcelos ended up in the embrace of Catholic clericalism; Revueltas broke with the Marxist clerisy. Which of the two was the true Christian?

Mexico D.F., 12 April 1979

LUIS CERNUDA: THE EDIFYING WORD

I

In 1961 the *Mercure de France* devoted an issue to Pierre Reverdy, who had recently died. Luis Cernuda wrote a few pages valuable not so much for what they say about Reverdy as for what they reveal, obliquely, about Cernuda himself: how he identifies poetic conscience with ethical purity, his taste for the essential word, which, not always justly, he set against what he called the sumptuousness of the Spanish and French traditions. But I recall that article not to stress the affinities between the French and the Spanish poet—though the influence of Reverdy on Cernuda would be worth pursuing—but because what Cernuda wrote three years ago on the destiny of dead poets seems today to have been thought and said about his own death: "What country suffers its poets with pleasure? Its living poets, I mean, since there is no country which doesn't adore its dead poets." Spain is no exception. Nothing is more natural than that the literary journals of the Iberian peninsula should publish homages to the poet: "Since Cernuda has died, long live Cernuda"; nothing is more natural, again, than that poets and critics, all together, cover with the same gray sediment of praises the oeuvre of a spirit which with admirable and inflexible obstinacy never stopped affirming his dissidence. When the poet is buried, we can discourse without risk about his work and make it say what it seems to us it ought to have said: where he wrote separation, we will read union: God where he said devil; homeland, not inhospitable land; soul, not body. And if "interpretation" is impossible, we will erase the forbidden words: rage, pleasure, nausea, boy, nightmare, solitude. . . . I do not want to suggest that all those who praise him try to whitewash what was black, nor that they do this entirely in bad faith. It's not a deliberate lie but a pious substitution. Perhaps without being aware, moved by a sincere desire to justify their admiration for a work which their conscience reproves, they transform a particular and unique truth—sometimes unbearable and repellent, like all that is truly fascinating—into a general and inoffensive truth, acceptable to all. Much of what has been written recently on Cernuda could have been written about any other poet. There have even been those who affirm that death has returned him to his native land ("When the dog is dead, rabies are at an end"). One critic, who claims he knows Cernuda's work well and admires it, does not hesitate to write: "The poet had a tragic fault: the inability to recognize any other kind of love but romantic love; thus conjugal love, paternal and filial love, were all closed doors for Cernuda." Another critic is of the view that the poet "has found a world in which reality and desire are in harmony." Has that writer asked himself what that paradise would be like, and what its angels and divinities would be?

Cernuda's work is an exploration of himself; a proud affirmation, in the last account not without the humility of its irreducible difference. He said it himself: "I have only tried, like

191